LEADERSHIP

OUTDATED THEORIES AND EMERGING

NON-TRADITIONAL LEADERSHIP

Dr. Warren D. Martin

Little Elephant Publishing

For more information contact:
Warrenmartin1956@gmail.com
warrenmartinleadership.com

ISBN - Paperback: 978-1-955129-21-3
ISBN - Hardback: 978-1-955129-22-0
ISBN - Ebook: 978-1-955129-23-7
ISBN - Audiobook: 978-1-955129-09-1

Book design by Warren Martin
Cover design by Warren Martin
Cover Photo by Christine Sponchia - christine-sponchia.pixels.com

First Edition: January 2024
Printed in the United States of America

Participant Quotes

"I think academics like to put these things into buckets. You know you're one of them, you're one of those… it's not the way I think. I don't know how many leaders do."

"There is no one formula or cookie cutter approach to effective leadership."

"The people graduating from business schools today have a completely different mindset than the people who graduate from business schools back in the 70s in terms of how they want to be treated and the things they want to do, what their expectations are, and how they think about work life balance."

"The world has changed a lot and leaders have to change with that world."

"I think the traditional MBA curriculum probably could use an update to the modern world and some schools probably do a better job of that than others. But I think there's still a lot of old school theory that is just pounded into people's head."

"We really don't have good leadership development programs."

"Effective leaders need to adapt to their circumstance" and *"There is no one formula or cookie cutter approach to effective leadership."*

TABLE OF CONTENTS

Foreword

There are many ways to look at leadership, its origin, application, and nature as an academic discipline. Some approach leadership's layers, as peeling an onion. Others study its angles, as facets of the discipline and its practice. Then there are those who look at its refracted light in the efforts of others and the culture within which they work.

When the needs of others are the focus, different leadership styles and their tools may prove more effective at any given point of time. But we all know that times change, and circumstances do, too. It is for this reason that one's leadership behavior should shift to meet individuals where they are to build their confidence and success (which equal leadership results and organizational success) from there. Flexibility, adaptability, and humility will take you far. Ah, yes, and one more thing—patience.

Take a good look at the pages that follow and find your past, present, and future leadership self within.

— Stacie L L Morgan, PhD, author of The Elephant Hunter: Speaking Truth in Organizations. https://www.staciellmorgan.com/

Abstract

The purpose of this qualitative study was to explore a phenomenon concerning why organizational leaders have transitioned from academically recommended leadership theories to their own non-traditional leadership practices. Existing research suggests that current leadership theories are outdated and not keeping pace with continual change, vast technological advancements, and expectations by stakeholders for transparency. The concept for this study was inspired in part by a combination of over 40-years of personal and professional observations and experience in leadership, and a personal theory that leaders do not practice traditional leadership theory as originally intended, but rather select various elements from numerous theories and merge them into a single leadership practice, also known as non-traditional leadership. The findings of this study suggested that all participants practiced non-traditional leadership. Continual change was recognized as an ongoing phenomenon, and leadership theories, or elements of theories, were considered outdated. Acceptance of change and adaptability was identified as necessary attributes for modern day successful leaders, and leaders who continued to practice traditional theory, did so out of fear of change. Additional research should be conducted to evaluate how widespread the practice of non-traditional leadership practices has spread and why leaders have chosen to ignore the recommended academic teachings of traditional leadership theories. Further research should be conducted concentrating on traditional leaders, in an effort to understand their motivations for following traditional leadership models.

Acknowledgements

I have been told that I have an interesting life, and I often jokingly reply "I just don't know what I want to do when I grow up. My parents divorced when I was six years old and my mother returned to her native Ireland, taking me with her. Four years later we returned to the United States, New York City, where I attended St. Stephens of Hungary elementary and started my struggles with education. I was placed two years behind my peers. I attended Power Memorial Academy high school, however dropped out in my junior year and joined the Army in 1975. Within a month I earned a GED, and during my 21-year career in the Army I attended college courses and earned my Bachelor's degree in 1993 from the University of New York.

My first and most important acknowledge is to my wife Debbie, who I met after joining the Army and has been with me ever since, encouraging me, supporting me, and standing by my side. My second acknowledge is to the United States Army, where I was introduced to leadership, and where during my career in the Infantry, Military Police, and Special Forces, I witnessed extraordinary leaders who demonstrated a variety of leadership methods and styles, and who mentored, influenced, and helped me immensely in gaining experience and developing my leadership skills.

I retired from the Army in 1996 and during the next 12 years worked for Domino's Pizza operating corporate owned stores and owned my own stores as a franchise. In 2010 I earned an MBA from the University of Michigan, and it was there that one of my professors, Dr. Rodney McGraw, expressed his observations concerning my expertise in leadership, and strongly suggested I pursue leadership as a specialty. Pursuing a PhD. at Northcentral University was a significant milestone in my life, and I believe I was very fortunate to be assigned Dr. Henry Luckel as my Dissertation Chair.

I am sincerely grateful for the support I've received from my wife Debbie, the countless friends, peers and leaders I've interacted with during my life. These individuals have provided a wide range of support and influence and have been instrumental in my journey up to this point. I am immensely proud to have known all the individuals who have been a part of my life and will always remember them as I move on to the next chapter in life.

Chapter 1

Introduction

Since the beginning of humanity, leadership has evolved through the ages, and although significant leadership research has been conducted and numerous theories developed during the past century, it has not produced a clearly universally defined and applicable theory that both researchers and leaders agree on (Allio, 2013; Bennis, 2013). The formal study of leadership began in the 1930s and has produced many leadership theories including the concept of transformational leadership in the 1970s by James MacGregor, however there is yet to be a single theory that academics can agree on (Allio, 2013; Bennett, 2009). Bennis (2013) and Latham (2014) suggested that current leadership theories may be outdated and that traditional leadership styles are not maintaining pace with the demands and needs of modern organizational environments.

Current leadership theory such as transformational or transactional implies that each leadership style be practiced independently, however there is extensive overlap and similarity between styles and many researchers continue to treat each as distinctive and separate (Allio, 2013; Van Dierendonck & Nuijten,

2011). A transformational leader inspires subordinates to perform for the good of an organization and focus on the long-term goals and performance while a transactional leader inspires using a goal-orientated system of leadership, however if one was to apply theory, a leader cannot practice both styles simultaneously (Ardichvili & Manderscheid, 2008; Safferstone, 2005). The suggestion by many researchers that leaders should practice a single leadership style results in restrictive leadership practices and limits the application of desired leadership traits (Derue & Wellman, 2009; Torres & Reeves, 2011). Leadership traits are behaviors exhibited by individuals for which Northouse (2013) identified intelligence, self-confidence, determination, integrity, and sociability as five major leadership traits desired for leaders engaged in any leadership capacity or style. Avolio, Walumbwa, and Weber (2009) and McCleskey (2014) suggested that traits such as intelligence, innovative thinking, and integrity are just some of the desired traits for a transformational leader, however these same traits are also desired of transactional and other leadership style leaders.

Before his death in 2014, the renowned pioneer in the field of leadership, Warren Bennis believed that leadership had been fundamentally changed due to globalization, technology, and digitization (Ardichvili & Manderscheid, 2008; George & Sims, 2007). The recommendation by Bennis has been echoed by other researchers including Latham (2014) and Dew, Enriquez, McFarlane, and Schroeder (2011) who have identified the phenomenon of an evolving and constant progression within society affecting all aspects of global interaction, economics, business, and organizational environments. Growing organizational dimensions, globalization, increased stakeholder involvement in organizational affairs, and changes within traditional business practices have created gaps in leadership and new requirements for leaders to possess an adaptive capacity and skill set to be effective (Latham, 2014). Hershey and Blanchard (1969) and McCleskey (2014) suggested that there is not an agreed upon method or leadership style that is considered best for influencing, and that specific situations call for different actions. Future leaders in all industries will be required to be more aware, involved, and interactive with their companies and employees, which will require alternative approaches to traditional leadership practices and the development of enhanced skills to effectively negotiate the continually changing organizational landscape (Ling, Simsek, Lubatkin, & Veiga, 2008; Rietsema & Watkins, 2012).

Formal leadership study had its beginning during the 1930s and has continued to be extensively researched (Allio, 2013; Bennett, 2009). Numerous leadership theories have been developed, however while there are multiple leadership theories being practiced, researchers have not agreed on which theory is the best theory (Allio, 2013; Bennett, 2009). Otte (2015) suggested that traditional leadership theory was developed for an industrial world without the vision for a future of globalized and collaborating network of organizations. Bennis (2014) suggested that due to the evolution of a technologically digital world and transparency, combined with requirements of leaders to lead across multiple dimensions, current leadership theories are not sufficient to accommodate current demands of today's organizational requirements.

Statement of the Problem

The changing organizational environments of the 21st century have resulted in a problem with the continued use of outdated leadership theories (Bennis, 2013; Latham, 2014). Contrary to the teachings of academics, numerous leaders no longer practice traditional leadership styles and have transitioned towards enhanced approaches including practicing several leadership styles simultaneously (Derue & Wellman, 2009; Kaigh, Driscoll, Tucker, & Lam, 2014; Srinivasan, 2010). According to Torres and Reeves (2014), and Sarros and Sarros (2011) leaders continuing to practice traditional leadership are less effective due to a lack of confidence, lack of adaptive capacity skills, and other factors. The general problem was the emergence of continual changing 21st century organizational environments combined with the practice of traditional leadership theories and styles that were not designed to address 21st century organizational issues associated with technology, globalization, and transparency, produces fewer effective leaders (Bennis, 2013; Latham, 2014; Rietsema & Watkins, 2012). According to McCleskey (2014) and Silva (2014), there is not a single effective leadership style, and there are conflicting perceptions and viewpoints regarding leadership by academia, academic researchers, and organizations where leadership is practiced.

The specific problem was that there was a lack of understanding of why organizational leaders have transitioned from academically recommended leadership theories to their own non-traditional leadership practices, a practice not yet associated with a leadership theory or model (Derue & Wellman, 2009; Fibuch, 2011; Kaigh, et al., 2014). This research produced data collected from participants who have recognized the issues that traditional leadership models have in 21st century organizations and are practicing new non-traditional leadership. Analysis of the participants' responses, perspectives, and decision-making process will produce insights clarifying why many existing theories are outdated and will contribute to developing new theory (Bennis, 2013; Fibuch, 2011; Latham, 2014).

Purpose of the Study

The purpose of this phenomenological qualitative study was to explore why organizational leaders have transitioned from academically recommended leadership theories to their own non-traditional leadership practices, a practice not yet associated with a leadership theory or model (Derue & Wellman, 2009; Fibuch, 2011; Kaigh, et al., 2014). Participant interviews provided data explaining why they ignored existing recommended leadership theories and what specifics, be it technological changes, organizational transparency, globalization, or other issues caused them to transition to their own non-traditional leadership practice (Bennis, 2013; Rietsema & Watkins, 2012). Data collected during the study contributed to emerging theory relating to non-traditional leadership practices and identified theories that are no longer relevant or meet the originally envisioned goals (Bennis, 2013; Latham, 2014).

The study produced research that added to existing literature and contributed to new emerging leadership theory (Bennis, 2013; Latham, 2014). The Creswell (2014) structured and semi-structured participant interview format was the most suitable method for gathering data because it enables contribution to existing or new theory and allows interviewees to present their own perspectives on the topic versus pre-identified answers to questions. A review of 83 qualitative studies by Bobby (2016) determined that there are no distinct guidelines to determine a recommended sample size for a qualitative study. Marshall, Cardon, Poddar, and Fontenot (2013) suggested that there is not a set or agreed upon sample size for qualitative research; however, they do cite several recommended sample-sizing guidelines including that of Creswell (2014) who suggested 15-20 participants for a qualitative study.

Theoretical/Conceptual Framework

The theoretical framework identified to support this study was based in part on the original research conducted in the 1970s by James MacGregor Burns related to his transformational leadership theory, and subsequent research years later by Bernard M. Bass and numerous other researchers (Bass, 1985; Bass & Bass, 2008; Bennett, 2009; Burns, 2010, Northouse, 2013). Based upon Burns' transformation leadership research, Bass developed the Bass transformational leadership theory that identified intellectual stimulation, individualized consideration, inspirational motivation, and idealized influence as four main elements of transformational leadership (Bass, 1985; Bass & Bass 2008). Leaders provide intellectual stimulation to their subordinates by encouraging independence and seeking new opportunities to accomplish goals (Bass, 1985; Bass & Bass 2008). Individualized consideration is provided through focusing on needs and serving as mentor, teacher, and motivator (Bass, 1985; Bass & Bass 2008). Inspirational motivation is demonstrated by a leader utilizing traits such as charisma to motivate groups and generating group purpose and meaning to a task (Bass, 1985; Bass & Bass 2008). Idealized influence is provided by leaders serving as role models and demonstrating traits such as honesty, trustworthiness, and enthusiasm (Bass, 1985; Bass & Bass 2008).

Kouses and Posner (2012) developed the five practices of exemplary leadership model that addressed the growing requirement for values centered leadership and leadership development (Naicker, Chikoko, & Mthiyane, 2014; Otte, 2015). Kouses and Posner's leadership model identified five essential elements and practices for leaders: model the way, inspire a shared vision, challenge the process, enable others to act, and encourage the heart. Model the way is a practice of setting the example, being the role model, creating opportunity and change, and taking the lead while creating relationships (Kouzes & Posner, 2017). Inspiring a shared vision is a practice of a leader having the ability to inspire others to share the vision of an organization while instilling the confidence that the mission can be accomplished by leaders (Kouzes & Posner, 2017).

Challenging the process is in essence challenging the status quo, accepting the possibility of failures while seeking challenging opportunities and innovative ways to pursue change leaders (Kouzes & Posner, 2017). Enabling others to act is a process of creating a positive working environment where leaders demonstrate their trust and willingness to work with others while also enabling them to exercise their own creativity and contributions to the organization leaders (Kouzes & Posner, 2017). Encourage the heart is the practice of leaders recognizing others for their achievements and providing awards, incentives, recognition, and sharing their success with other leaders (Kouzes & Posner, 2017).

Northouse (2013) identified intelligence, self-confidence, determination, integrity, and sociability as the major traits of a leader. Intelligence is considered to be reasoning ability and self-confidence is the ability of a leader to have confidence in their own skills and competencies (Northouse, 2013). Determination is demonstrating persistence and personal drive to accomplish a task (Northouse, 2013). Integrity is a trait of possessing trustworthiness and honesty, and sociability is the leader's ability to establish a rapport of being approachable and someone who can interact on a personal and social level with others (Northouse, 2013).

Avolio (2009) and Ling (2008) suggested that transformational leadership and its associated traits have emerged as the dominant leadership style. Burns (2012), Bennett (2009), Latham (2014), Northouse (2013) and Thompson (2012) suggested that the traits of leadership, including Kouzes and Posner's five practices of exemplary leadership, are not restricted to one single leadership style and can be practiced across multiple leadership styles (Kouzes & Posner, 2017). Kouzes and Posner (2012) suggested that leaders have evolved and practice multiple leadership styles simultaneously, evident by the practice of common traits found across numerous leadership styles.

Research Questions

The purpose of this phenomenological qualitative study utilizing semi-structured research questions was to explore and collect date regarding organizational leaders and their decision to ignore academically recommended leadership theory, and transition to practicing their own modified non-traditional leadership style, a practice not yet associated with a leadership theory or model.

Q1. What events or phenomenon, if any, are causing leaders to practice non-traditional leadership?

Q2. How are stakeholders' expectations, if any, influencing leadership transition towards non-traditional leadership practices?

Q3. What concepts or other elements of traditional leadership theory, if any, are practiced within non-transitional leadership practices?

The use of existing literature and participants for the research was discussed, and utilized a combination of unstructured interviews, observations, and conversations as tools used in the research design (Anfara & Mertz, 2015; Edmonds & Kennedy, 2017).

Nature of the Study

The qualitative method of research was utilized for this study and given that the research topic was related to a behavior, it did not require experimentation since measurable numeric or statistical research cannot be used (Anfara & Mertz, 2015; Creswell, 2014). The use of qualitative research is defined as a focus on people in their natural settings and describing their settings in their own words (Edmonds & Kennedy, 2017). Qualitative research also addresses either the creating or generating of new theory or hypotheses, achieving an understanding of the issues, or developing detailed stories to describe a phenomenon (Yates & Leggett, 2016). The phenomenological approach to qualitative study identifies lived experiences and takes advantage of personal face-to-face interviews to extract data (Willis, Sullivan-Bolyai, Knafl & Cohen, 2016).

The research study did not require experimentation. The research topic was related to behavior practiced by individual leaders.

The qualitative method of research was identified as the most appropriate for this research (Donnelly, 2017).

Significance of the Study

Kaigh et al, (2014) suggested that contrary to the existing practice of traditional leadership theories, leaders are transitioning from academically recommended leadership theories to their own non-traditional leadership practices. There is a lack of understanding as to why this emerging phenomenon has occurred, and there is continued investment in educating leaders with theories that may no longer be adequate to meet the continual changing organizational environments (Bennis, 2013; Latham, 2014). The data collected during this study supported and contributed to Bennis (2013) and Latham's (2014) recommendations relating to understanding why leaders have transitioned towards alternative approaches to leadership, understanding new emerging non-traditional leadership practices, and identified theories that are no longer relevant or meet the originally envisioned goals.

Definition of Key Terms

The following list of terms is critical or relevant to the topic of leadership and may not be common knowledge to persons not familiar with organizational leadership.

Adaptive Capacity. The term adaptive capacity is used in leadership to identify a trait or characteristic of an individual who possesses the ability to be resilient and quickly and effectively adapt to expected and unexpected change in the organizational environment. Leaders who possess an adaptive capacity can envision change, embracing transparency, and adapting on the move as events occur (Bennis, 2013; Latham, 2014).

Authentic Leadership. The authentic leader is credited with possessing values, heart, purpose, self-discipline and an ability to foster relationships (George & Sims, 2007). The authentic leader is also a person who is perceived as having credibility and character and demonstrates a consistency of integrity and ability to engage people while developing a culture of trust within an organization (Hamm, 2011).

Autocratic leadership. Autocratic leadership is an extreme form of transactional leadership, where leaders exercise complete control over subordinates. Autocratic leadership is used in crises and the military where top commanders are responsible for quickly making complex decisions, which allows troops to focus their attention and energy on performing their allotted tasks and missions (Faerman, McGrath, Quinn, & St. Clair, 2007; United States Army, 2006).

Charismatic/value-based leadership. Charismatic/value-based leadership reflects the ability to inspire, to motivate, and to expect high performance from others based on strongly held core values. This kind of leadership includes being visionary, inspirational, self-sacrificing, trustworthy, decisive, and performance oriented (Northouse, 2013).

Competencies. Competence develops from a balanced combination of institutional schooling, self-development, realistic training, and professional experience. Building competence follows a systematic and gradual approach, from mastering individual competencies, to applying them in concert and tailoring them to the situation at hand. Leading people by giving them a complex task helps them develop the confidence and will to take on progressively more difficult challenges (United States Army, 2006).

Competing Values Framework (CVF). Competing values is a broadly applicable model that fosters successful leadership, improves organizational effectiveness, and promotes value creation. The premise of the CVF is that there are four basic competing values within every enterprise: Collaborate, Create, Compete, and Control (Faerman, McGrath, Quinn, & St. Clair, 2007).

Confidence. Confidence is the faith that leaders place in their abilities to act properly in any situation, even under stress and with little information. Leaders who know their own capabilities and believe in themselves are confident. Self-confidence grows from professional competence (United States Army, 2006).

Direct Leadership. The United States Army defines direct leadership as face-to-face or first-line leadership. It generally occurs in organizations where subordinates are accustomed to seeing their leaders all the time: teams and squads; sections and platoons; companies, batteries, troops, battalions, and squadrons. The direct leader's span of influence may range from a handful to several hundred people (United States Army, 2006).

Ethical Leadership. An accepted definition for ethics is that it focuses on the kinds of morals and values that individuals and members of society find to be appropriate and desirable (Northouse, 2013). The subject of ethics is also said to be a central issue to leadership and the process of influencing, engaging followers to accomplish goals and having an impact on the establishment of an organization's values (Northouse, 2013).

Five practices of exemplary leadership. The five practices of exemplary leadership are a transformational leadership model developed by Kouses and Posner. Model the way, inspire a shared vision, challenge the process, enable others to act, and encourage the heart are the five practices that Kouses and Posner identified as essential elements and practices that leaders should develop and use to ensure success (Kouzes & Posner, 2012).

Knowledge management. Knowledge management, also referred to as KM, has been an identified research field since the 1990's and has also been used and viewed in conjunction with other disciplines and names for an extended period of time (Koenig & Srikantaiah, 2004). Knowledge management has been defined by the American Productivity and Quality Center (APQC) as an emerging set of strategies and approaches to create, safeguard and put into use a wide range of knowledge assets such as information and people (Koenig & Srikantaiah, 2004).

Laissez-faire leadership. The commonly accepted definition for laissez-faire leadership is defined as a leader that takes a *hands-off* approach. The leader abdicates responsibility, delays decisions, gives no feedback, and makes little efforts to help followers satisfy their needs. There is no exchange with followers or attempt to help them grow (Northouse, 2013).

Organizational Culture. Organizational culture can generally be defined as the values, behaviors, and beliefs that are practiced by an organization (Curphy, Ginnett & Hughes, 2009; Northouse, 2013).

Organizational leadership. Organizational leadership is defined as that which encompasses the traditional traits of leadership and the possession of learned skills and experience, providing the leader the ability to lead and manage across the multiple complex levels of organizational structures (Curphy, Ginnett & Hughes, 2009; Northouse, 2013).

Path-Goal Theory. Path-Goal Theory is a concept that leaders will provide or ensure the availability of valued rewards for followers (the "goal") and then help them find the best way of getting there (the "path") (Curphy, Ginnett & Hughes, 2009).

Relationship management. Relationship management is a process that facilitates empathy and self-management and defines leaders as being attuned to people's feelings and able to guide them in positive emotional directions (Kouzes & Posner, 2012).

Servant leadership. Servant Leadership is a philosophy in which a leader interacts with others with the goal of achieving authority rather than power over subordinates. The authority figure intends to promote the well-being of those around him/her. Servant leadership involves the individual demonstrating the characteristics of empathy, listening, stewardship, and commitment to personal growth toward others (Faerman, McGrath, Quinn, & St. Clair, 2007).

Strategic leadership. Strategic leadership is the ability to anticipate, envision, maintain flexibility, and empower others to create strategic change as necessary. Multifunctional in nature, strategic leadership involves managing through others, managing an entire enterprise rather than a functional subunit, and coping with change that continues to increase in the 21st century (Hitt, Hoskisson & Ireland, 2012).

Transactional leadership. Transactional leadership is defined as simple exchanges between leaders and followers for attaining goals, giving promotions, bonuses or other transactional exchanges for performance (Northouse, 2013).

Transformational leadership. Transformational leadership is defined as a method where the leaders in a sense transformed themselves, and through changes in their own behaviors and actions connected and interacted with their followers creating higher levels of motivation, morality and ultimately performance outcomes (Northouse, 2013).

Summary

The purpose of this study was to explore why organizational leaders have transitioned towards their own non-traditional leadership practices. The qualitative method of research was selected as the most appropriate for this leadership research study. Donnelly (2017) suggested that behavioral research related to behavior does not require experimentation. Barnham (2015) and Donnelly (2017) suggested that a combination of unstructured interviews, grounded theory, observations, and conversations, are the recommended tools to be used in a qualitative research design. Qualitative research provides flexibility and is less restrictive, allowing a broad view of possible outcomes (Donnelly, 2017; Barnham, 2015). According to Anfara and Mertz (2015) and Fowler (2014) quantitative research is a viable method for providing numerical and statistical research.

CHAPTER 2

LITERATURE REVIEW

The literature review addressed the historical perspective of existing leadership theory and the emerging trends towards non-traditional practices. The majority of the literature was a review of scholarly peer-reviewed articles, journals, dissertations, and books utilizing EBSCO Host™, ProQuest™, Google Scholar™ Northcentral University library databases, and Academy of Management resources. This literature review covered a review of the history of leadership, traits, theories, and styles, and the sub-themes of continual change, conflicting and outdated theories, and the trait approach to leadership.

Leadership History

Leadership is considered an important area of study while also being an area that lacks universal understanding and agreement (Northouse, 2013). The formal study in leadership is a topic of interest that began in the past century (Allio, 2013). The study of leadership has evolved during the past century with continually increasing interest in the research of leadership. One example is the leadership quarterly, a scholarly journal founded by Bernard Bass in

1990, which has contributed over 800 manuscripts to the topic of leadership (Dionne et al., 2014). The topic of leadership has been one of the most taught subjects at business schools throughout the United States and the world during the last fifty years (Collinson & Tourish, 2015).

Leadership, even in its most basic form, has been in existence within civilizations since the first family unit, clan, village, and other organized groups that came into existence (Allio, 2013; Celarent, 2014). Early civilizations like the Phoenicians made several contributions to the world including navigational techniques, advanced glass making, and the phonetic alphabet (Gore, 2004). The Greeks and Romans are credited with the introduction of the democratic type of government, architecture, aqueducts, calendar, the arts, the census and countless other contributions (Chase, Jacob, J., Jacob, M., Perry, & Von Laue, 2013). The entrepreneurial drive and accomplishments of these and other societies is evidence of the existence of some form of organized leadership and the continual advancement of leadership throughout history (Anderson, Curley & Formica, 2010).

During the last century, leadership has evolved from a practice, or something people did, to a defined process of research that has produced numerous leadership theories and styles (Dionne, et al., 2014). Leadership studies conducted in the 1930s by the University of Iowa focused on identifying what was believed to be the best leadership practice (Bhatti, Maitlo, Shaikh, Hashmi, & Shaikh, 2012). The research conducted by Kurt Lewin identified laissez-faire, democratic, and autocratic as the three main leadership practices (Bhatti et al., 2012). The laissez-faire leader is considered to be someone who relinquishes control and responsibility to others, while the autocratic leader autocratic leader maintains a controlled environment, centered decision making, dictatorial system of work for followers, and limits the participation of followers (Bhatti et al., 2012). The democratic leadership style was determined to be more effective for positive employee attitudes and morale, which was accomplished through collaborating with followers, delegation, and participation (Omilion-Hodges & Wieland, 2016; Smothers, 2011).

Leadership research in the 1940s and 1950s by Ohio State Leadership Studies identified problems associated with organizations, groups, and the role of followers related to leadership (Stogdill, 1950). During the period of the Ohio research observations were made about a developing move from authoritarian leadership practices towards a transactional style approach (Omilion-Hodges & Wieland, 2016). The Ohio State studies conducted by Stogdill identified two main elements associated with leadership practices, one being initiating of structure and the other being consideration (Rowold, 2011). A leaders' ability to initiate structure within the organization and responsibilities for follower's impacted task-related goals and was effective in profitability and performance (Rowold, 2011). Consideration impacted meeting follower's relationships and needs, encouraged positive aspects such as open communication, respect, and trust between the followers and leaders (Rowold, 2011). Consideration was determined to be the most effective element related to follower commitment and performance satisfaction (Ayman & Korabik, 2010).

In the 1960s, the University of Michigan conducted studies which were comparable to the Ohio State studies from the late 1940s and early 1950s. The purpose of the Michigan studies, conducted by Likert, was to establish leadership effectiveness (Gregoire & Arendt, 2014; Northouse, 2013). The research produced production-centered and employee-centered types of behavior-orientated leadership styles (Ayman & Korabik, 2010; Northouse, 2013). Production-centered leaders focused on technical aspects whereas employee-centered leaders focused on relationships. Leaders who focused on employees had higher rates of group performance and job satisfaction. Leaders who focused on production resulted in low satisfaction and production (Gregoire & Arendt, 2014; Yukl, 2012).

The study of leadership has produced and will continue to produce valued research, however, during the past century a phenomenon has emerged that also focuses on followers and the impact they have on organizational leadership and success (Allio, 2013). The modern follower has gained power, control, knowledge, and empowerment within their organizational environments (Allio, 2013; Carter, 2013). The modern follower is tech savvy, up to date, and involved in every aspect of their industry specialization (Allio, 2013; Carter, 2013). Leaders are no longer just fulfilling a leadership role; they are required to provide the guidance and direction to followers to develop and maintain their skills to implement and sustain market performance and relationships with customer, counterparts, and alliances (Allio, 2013; Carter, 2013).

Leadership Theories

The formal study of leadership dates back to the 1930s and since that time, researchers have produced numerous leadership theories and styles (Allio, 2013; Bennett, 2009). A twentieth-century pioneer in the study of leadership, Warren Bennis, wrote in his 1985 book *On Becoming a Leader* about leaders transitioning from traditional leadership and focusing on gaining control, to a more non-traditional method of inspiring followers (Bennis, 2009). The Bennis approach to leadership was a change from traditional thinking and presented the way toward more of a trait approach where leaders provided vision, passion, integrity and trust (Bennis, 2009). Bennis's approach to leadership inspired or enhanced similar research like that of Kouzes and Posner *The Leadership Challenge* series of books that emphasized credibility, morals, values, ethics, and interaction (Kouzes & Posner, 2017). The ability of leaders to build teams, recognize the contributions of others and celebrate the success of individuals and teams was an important dynamic required by leaders to be successful (Kouzes & Posner, 2017).

The Great Man Theory

A precursor to the formal study of leadership was the Great Man theory. The Great Man theory was not necessarily based on research but more on opinions and personal perspectives of the times. In the 1840s, Thomas Carlyle, a writer from Scotland, introduced the concept that leaders were born and not made, a concept that developed into theory and followed in principle into the twentieth century (Hoffman, Lyons, Maldagen-Youngjohn, & Woehr, 2011).

The hypothesis of the Great Man Theory is that leaders are made and not made, trained, or developed, hence the saying "A born leader" (Allio, 2013; Cawthon, 1996). Reinforcing the Great Man theory was an 1869 study by Galton that claimed certain attributes of leaders are genetically passed on from one generation to another (Lee, 2011). Thomas Carlyle believed that individuals personal traits, predetermined characteristics, and inherent ability, produced heroes who rose to challenges and leadership roles (Hoffman et al., 2011). The Great Man theory, in essence, was an assumption that only certain individuals possessed required characteristic and traits that would empower them to be leaders (Bass & Bass, 2008). The Great Man Theory maintained prominence through the 1940s in part due to its exclusion of women from leadership roles (Cawthon, 1996).

Trait Theories

The Great Man theory and trait theorist believed that individuals were born with certain leadership traits and that these traits could not be learned nor gained through education or training (Northouse, 2013). The 1930s and 1940s brought a spinoff of the Great Man theory and transitioned towards a modified viewpoint of trait theory (Northouse, 2013). Individual attributes were the focus of the trait approach to leadership study, which suggested that there were distinctive characteristics and personality traits that made up an individual's ability to be a leader (Colbert, Judge, Choi & Wang, 2012).

A significant difference with the new views of trait theory was that it presented the concept that individuals could be either be born or made if they could learn the traits to be a good leader (Fleenor, 2011). Stogdill's 1948 study identified alertness, insight, responsibility, initiative, persistence, self-confidence, and sociability as some of the dominant leadership traits (Northouse, 2013). In 1959 Mann's study added adjustment, dominance, extroversion, conservatism and masculinity to the list of traits (Northouse, 2013). Stogdill produced another study in 1974 in which achievement, tolerance, influence, and cooperativeness were added as additional traits (Northouse, 2013). Further studies as noted in figure 1 added masculinity, dominance, drive, motivation, confidence, cognitive ability and task knowledge to a list of leadership traits (Northouse, 2013).

Figure 1. Studies of leadership Traits

Stogdill (1948)	Mann (1959)	Stogdill (1974)	Lord, DeVader, and Alliger (1986)	Kirkpatrick and Locke (1991)
Intelligence	Intelligence	Achievement	Intelligence	Drive
Alertness	Masculinity	Persistence	Masculinity	Motivation
Insight	Adjustment	Insight	Dominance	Integrity
Responsibility	Dominance	Initiative		Confidence
Initiative	Extroversion	Self-confidence		Cognitive ability
Persistence	Conservatism	Responsibility		Task knowledge
Self-confidence		Cooperativeness		
Sociability		Tolerance		
		Influence		
		Sociability		

Figure 1. Studies of Leadership Traits. Reprinted from *Leadership: Theory and practice* (p. 18), by P. Northouse, 2013, Thousand Oaks, CA: Sage Publications. Copyright 2007 by Sage Publications.

One of the primary focuses of trait theorists was on ascertaining the specific traits of leaders (Cruz, Nunes, & Pinheiro, 2011). Trait theory established core concepts for leadership research, however, it did not consider the leader-follower aspect and the interactions between leaders and followers (Cruz et al., 2011). The development of trait theory, and what it lacked, provided the foundation for the research that began in the 1940s on behavior theories and other leadership theories that would follow (Cruz et al., 2011).

Behavioral Theories

One of the differences between trait theory and behavior theory is that the study of behavior theory focused on individual's actions instead of certain traits an individual possesses (Gupta & Singh, 2013). During the late 1940s, there was a transition from trait theory toward behavior types of leadership (Cruz et al., 2011). In the 1930s, the University of Iowa conducted a study of leadership that identified laissez-faire, democratic, and authoritarian as categories of leadership behavior (Schuh, Zhang, & Tian, 2013).

Laissez-faire behavior was considered by many to be a negative approach to leadership utilizing a hands-off approach (Northouse 2013). The positive intent of laissez-faire behavior was to empower and delegate responsibility while establishing the necessary peer to peer communication that would achieve an organizations' objectives (Bass & Bass, 2008; Northouse 2013). Democratic behavior was a method by which there was communication with followers who were included in the decision-making process (Northouse 2013). Authoritarian behavior was a method by which followers were given direct task by a leader and the expectation was for followers to do as instructed (Northouse 2013; Schuh et al., 2013).

Contingency Theory

The Contingency theory was developed in 1967 by Fiedler and theorized that specific situations would dictate which type of response and leadership was required to address the situation with a successful reaction (Fiedler, 1967; Prindle, 2012). Contingency theory was a departure from behavioral and trait leadership models and began an approach that suggested, based on organizational requirements, that leaders should use different leadership styles and approaches (Andibo, 2012). The Contingency theory is one of the more largely researched leadership theories and asserted that organizations should match a leaders' skills with styles and psychological attitude (Northouse, 2013). The application of contingency theory was to identify organizational situations and place leaders possessing pre-determined leadership traits in leadership positions (Gray, 2013; Northouse, 2013).

Situational Theories

The situational leadership theory was developed in the 1960s by Blanchard based on a concept that different situations would require varying responses (Blanchard & Hersey, 1996). The theory suggested that leaders had to adapt their leadership approach based on the level of individual follower development (Blanchard & Hersey, 1996). The theory further suggested that based on the maturity level of followers, the leader should match the appropriate decision-making style, either delegating, participating, telling, or selling, to the followers' particular skill level (Northouse, 2013).

Stogdill's 1948 study was instrumental in beginning a shift from the trait approach to leadership toward situational leadership (Northouse, 2013). Stogdill continued his research and in 1974 produced a follow-up study that suggested that traits were not a determinant of a leader's effectiveness. The study suggested that while leaders may have shared common traits, it was their ability to adapt to situations and apply appropriate and different leadership styles in response to the situations, which in turn would produce desired results (Northouse, 2013).

Authoritarian - Autocratic Leadership

One of the earliest established leadership styles, possibly the first, can arguably be the authoritarian style, practiced by the autocratic leader (Flynn, 2015). During the 1930s a study was conducted by the University of Iowa with the purpose to identify the preferred leadership style (Smothers, 2011). The study, led by Kurt Lewin, determined that there were three commonly practiced leadership styles, the autocratic, democratic, and laissez-faire. Autocratic leaders have been defined as being closed-minded, power-orientated, controlling, and in some contexts considered an example of transactional leadership (Bass, 2008; Giltinane, 2013). Authoritarian type rule has been exercised by leaders over nations for centuries in the form of monarchies, religions, dictatorships, and communism (Gandhi & Przeworski, 2013).

Autocratic leaders are not limited to repressive regimes and continue to practice in various organizations. A characteristic of the autocratic leadership style is that it is more of a method utilized by leaders to dictate, tell, or demand their subordinates to perform tasks (Elqadri, Priyono, Suci, & Chandra, 2015). The authoritarian or autocratic leader is portrayed as overbearing and bossy, and they gain their control over followers with rules, demands, threats, and punishment (Flynn, 2015).

The role of followers is to follow instructions without question and non-participation or input to operational tasks (Flynn, 2015). This approach ignores input by others and provides an organization with a direct direction of focus, however, it can also create an environment where the autocratic leader is disliked by subordinates (Bass 2008; Elqadri et al., 2015). Organizations with autocratic leaders tend to have high turnover rates, absenteeism, and follower unhappiness (Flynn, 2015).

The success of the autocratic leader has been attributed in part to the icon or image status of the individual in which followers have an established trust and reverence for the leader, or in other cases fear of the leader (Bush, Erlich, Prather & Zeira, 2016). Another characteristic of the autocratic leaders is their refusal for weighting their subordinate's views, opinions, or decisions that impact their organization (Bhatti, Murta Maitlo, Shaikh, Hashmi & Shaikh, 2012). The University of Iowa studies by Lewin suggested that autocratic leadership created environments of aggressiveness, hostility, and lack of motivation (Bhatti et al., 2012).

Although the autocratic leader can be disliked, subordinates do perform well and reinforce a perception that well-liked leaders are not as efficient as disliked autocratic leaders (Bass, 2008; Schoel, Bluemke, Mueller & Stahlberg, 2011). Autocratic leaders provide focus, structure, and rewards; however, they can be responsible for creating fear and being abusive (Bass, 2008; Schoel et al., 2011). Research by Al-Khasawneh and Futa (2013) suggested that the practice of autocratic leadership did not necessarily have a negative impact relating to relationships whereas other leadership styles such as democratic do have a positive influence on followers.

Path-Goal Theory

Path-Goal leadership is based on a theory that followers are provided goals through value rewards, and the leaders provide the best method, or path, to accomplish the goals (Hughes, Curphy &

Ginnett, 2015). Path-Goal leadership was developed by House in the early 1970s in collaboration with Evans, Dessler, and Mitchell (House, 1996; Phillips & Phillips, 2016). An element of path-goal theory is the premise that leaders should increase the motivation, satisfaction, and performance of followers through communicating, rewarding, and eliminating obstacles that could interfere with accomplishing the goals (Hollenbeck, DeRue & Nahrgang, 2015; House, 1996). In addition to meeting leader and follower goals, the use of path-goal leadership was intended to meet organizational goals (Yukl, 2012).

Path-Goal is a behavioral or situational theory that blends elements of leader behaviors, characteristics of followers, and situations (Hollenbeck, DeRue & Nahrgang, 2015). Path-Goal is an alternative approach to established leadership theory that did not allow for different approaches to situational change, and addressed a belief that there is not a leadership style that can be applied to every situation (MacDonald & Luque, 2013). Path-Goal theory was developed to create an understanding of how to analyze, predict, and influence the behavior of followers (MacDonald & Luque, 2013).

House identified four leadership behaviors, or styles, that he believed to be applicable to leadership situations: achievement-oriented, directive, supportive, and participative (Phillips & Phillips, 2016). House suggested that leaders should be flexible and open to adjusting their leadership style and behavior based on each situation (MacDonald & Luque, 2013). The leader should not only adjust their own behavior on the situation, but also on the particular characteristics of the follows and the task (Saccomano & Pinto-Zipp, 2011).

The achievement-orientated leader is capable of setting challenging and demanding goals that result in followers performing at their best performance. The leader expresses confidence in the skills and abilities of followers' performance and results. Achievement-orientated behavior is most effective when results can be evaluated and measured (House, 1996; Saccomano & Pinto-Zipp, 2011).

A leader would use the directive approach with followers in situations where assigned jobs are vague or uncertain (House, 1996; Saccomano & Pinto-Zipp, 2011). Specific assignments are given to followers by the leaders with detailed instructions on both what and how to accomplish the task (House, 1996; Saccomano & Pinto-Zipp, 2011). The leader provides clear direction which in turn instills follower motivation and satisfaction (House, 1996; Saccomano & Pinto-Zipp, 2011).

The participative leader projects confidence, trust, and respect with followers (House, 1996; Saccomano & Pinto-Zipp, 2011). A participative leader solicits follower input and expertise during the evaluation process of tasks or projects (House, 1996; Saccomano & Pinto-Zipp, 20110. Through the participative process, followers develop self-confidence and credibility in their respective performance areas (House, 1996; Saccomano & Pinto-Zipp, 2011).

The practice of being a supportive leader is generally best utilized in situations where there is stressful and physically demanding task (House, 1996; Saccomano & Pinto-Zipp, 2011). A leader who demonstrates actions that concern the welfare of followers is considered a supportive leader (House, 1996; Saccomano & Pinto-Zipp, 2011). A leader who demonstrates concern for followers' welfare is said to produce follower's willingness to be more productive in an effort to please their leader (House, 1996; Saccomano & Pinto-Zipp, 2011).

Figure 2. Path-Goal Leadership

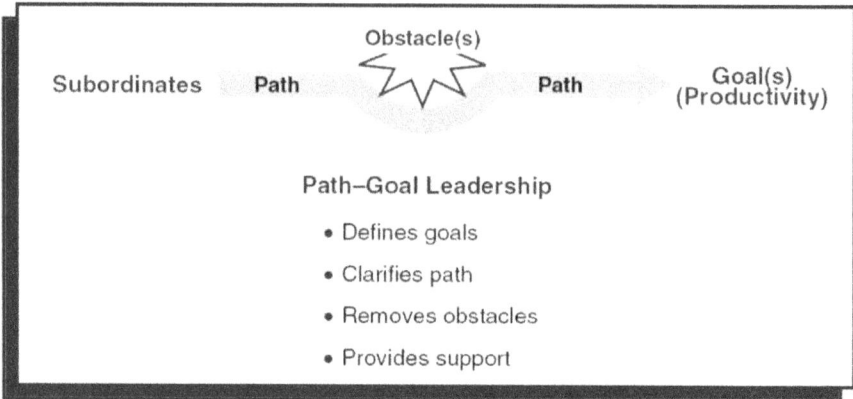

Figure 2. Path-Goal Leadership. Reprinted from *Leadership: Theory and practice* (p. 128), by P. Northouse, 2013, Thousand Oaks, CA: Sage Publications. Copyright 2007 by Sage Publications.

Transactional Theory

The theory of transactional leadership is credited to Max Weber who introduced it in 1947 (McCleskey, 2014). The transactional model contains management by exception, contingent reward, and goal achievement (Bass, 1997). Transactional leadership is identified as a method of exchanging behaviors by leaders and followers that generate rewards. A transactional leader gains performance of followers through contingent rewarding (Humphrey, 2013).

Northouse (2013) defined transactional leadership as a simple exchange between leaders and followers for attaining goals, giving promotions, bonuses or other transactional exchanges for performance. Transactional leadership is an exchange process between followers and leaders (McCleskey, 2014; Rowold, 2014). Transactional leadership as a style is centered on authority and legitimacy established within organizations (Hargis, Watt, & Piotrowski, 2011). The focus of transactional leadership style is centered on assignments, performance, task orientated goals and generally is focused on the day-to-day operations within organizations (Lord, Day, Zaccaro, Avolio & Eagly, 2017).

Transactional leadership has also been defined as a method for taking action or reacting to problems and rewarding individuals who exceeded or achieved objectives (Holmberg, Fridell, Arnesson, & Bäckvall, 2008). Ardichvili and Manderscheid (2008) asserted that transactional leadership is the predominant managerial practice between followers and their leaders and involves exchanges of mutual values and benefits. Bass (1999) suggested that transactional leaders assisted followers with fulfilling their own interest by rewarding the follower's expectations, clarifying their objectives and responsibilities.

Bass and Bass (2008) suggested that before the introduction of transformational leadership, leaders utilized contingent reward as their main tool to create effective follower performance. Bass (1985) and Burns (1978) stated that one task of transactional leadership is to gain job performance by followers, which is achieved through the use of contingent reward to fulfill the expectations and needs of the followers. Research conducted by

Epitropaki and Martin (2013) suggested that in organizations where unsure and unpredictable events occurred, there was positive relationships between followers and transformational leaders, whereas in stable and predictable organizations, transactional leaders and their followers experienced positive outcomes (Humphrey, 2013). Transactional leadership provides recognition for successful performance and a clear expectation of what the performance should be (Humphrey, 2013).

Martínez-Córcoles and Stephanou (2017) studied transactional leadership and how the transactional method impacted safety in military parachute operations. The study of 161 military parachutists suggested that transactional directed activities fulfilled positive safety standards and performance. The study suggested that the application of transactional tasks and rewards, when applied to safety procedures, was embraced by participants.

Behavioral, contingency, and trait theories are associated with transactional leadership. Transactional leaders are reward and task focused, and assist followers with obtaining their own gains and interest (Rowold, 2011). The transactional leader is aligned with the status quo, avoids taking chances, and utilizes a system of rewards and agreements to motivate followers (Sadeghi & Pihie, 2012).

Transformational Theory

Transformational leadership is considered to be the most researched, studied, and possibly most practiced leadership theory of the past forty years (Dionne et al., 2014). The initial concept of transformational leadership is said to have been developed by James

MacGregor Burns in the 1970s and later developed by Bass in 1985 (Deschamps, Rinfret, Lagacé & Privé, 2016; Lord et al., 2017).

Transformational leadership is defined as a method where the leaders in a sense transformed themselves, and through changes in their own behaviors and actions connected and interacted with their followers creating higher levels of motivation, morality and ultimately performance outcomes (Lord et al., 2017). Transformational leadership has also been defined as employing a dual dynamic between leaders and followers with a goal to attain organizational results (Alsaeedi & Male, 2013).

Northouse (2013) asserted that the principle theory of transformational leadership is the role that leadership is concerned with the transformation of organizations. The ability of leaders to envision the need for, and to implement change within organizational structure is critical to successful performance and outcomes (Northouse, 2013). Leadership development has utilized a shared vision approach to transformational leadership, a sharp contrast compared to other leadership theories like transactional theory where focus is strictly focused on single exchanges or concepts (Balyer, 2012).

The style of transformational leadership is aligned on legitimacy and authority established within organizations (Hargis, Watt, & Piotrowski, 2011). In contrast, the style of transactional leadership is focused on assignments, performance, task orientated goals, and generally is focused with the day to day operations within organizations (Aga, 2016). The effect of transformational and transactional leadership styles practiced within organizations was studied by Ejene and Abasilim (2013). Their research of a

2006 study in Chile suggested that the behavior of transformational leaders had a compelling and decisive effect on organizational success. The study focused on how leadership style influenced employee performance at small sized organizations. Results showed that transformational leaders produced positive employee performance, whereas laissez-faire and transactional leadership created negative employee impact within organizational performance (Ejene & Abasilim, 2013).

Transformational leaders possess a distinguishing characteristic setting them apart from other leadership theories. Transformational leaders focus on traditional and hierarchical positions of power best suited for their operating environment (Schuh, Zhang, & Tian, 2013). Transformational leaders are engaged in self-focused concepts such as self-esteem, self-confidence, and self-efficacy (Calik, Sezgin, Kavgaci, & Cagatay, 2012). Transformational leaders are individuals who enable an environment of continual learning (Balyer, 2012).

Transformational leaders are characterized by engaging in the recruitment and grooming of followers, and providing environments that promote a shared vision (Chism & Pang, 2014). Transformational leadership impacts organizational effectiveness via the applications of strategic human resource management (Pongpearchan, 2016). The transformational leader employs intellectual stimulation of followers to engage them in the organization's mission and completion of goals (Pongpearchan, 2016).

Leaders who demonstrate transformational characteristics are developers of groups of connected followers engaged in shared vision and organizational success (Drago-Severson, 2012). A transformational leader has an awareness of how to motivate followers through fulfilling their needs (Drago-Severson, 2012). Transformational leaders possess abilities to decrease concern and worry in their followers (Ishikawa, 2012). Transformational leaders have higher expectations for themselves and their followers and have a skill at motivating and engaging followers to exceed their own perceived capabilities (Hauserman, Ivankova, & Stick, 2013; Whitenack & Swanson, 2013).

Transformational leadership has been identified as possessing four elements or sub-components: idealized influence, inspirational motivation, intellectual stimulation, and individualized consideration (Deschamps, Rinfret, Lagacé, & Privé, 2016). Idealized influence addresses transformational leaders possessing charisma and who are seen by followers as role models (Deinert et al., 2015). Idealized influence by a leader demonstrates core values, principles, convictions, and willingness to take risk, which in turn influences followers to develop trust in the leader (Deinert et al., 2015). Idealized influence can be an approach to negative workplace situations where a leader's positive role and optimism inspires followers (Zdaniuk & Bobocel, 2015)

Inspirational motivation addresses the ability of a leader to motivate and inspire confidence in followers (Deinert et al., 2015). A transformational leader should be skilled at projecting enthusiasm and optimism (Deinert et al., 2015). A Transformational leader should be capable of demonstrating vision, expectations, and communication skills to influence and inspire followers to succeed in goal achievement (Deinert et al., 2015).

Intellectual stimulation is demonstrated by the transformation leader through involving followers in the planning and decision process (Deinert et al., 2015). The leader provides vision to followers and includes them in the organizational mission and goals (Deinert et al., 2015). The leader allows independence and creativity and solicits innovation from followers to identify and solve problems (Deinert et al., 2015).

Individualized consideration is the demonstrated efforts by the leader to address follower's concerns (Deinert et al., 2015). The concerns of followers can be financial, job satisfaction, work environment, or any number of issues concerning the follower's well-being (Deinert et al., 2015). The skill required of a leader is the ability to recognize follower's concerns, both real and perceived by the followers, and the ability to communicate on a personal level with followers (Deinert et al., 2015).

In 1987, Kouses and Posner (2012) developed a transformational leadership model that identified five practices. The five practices in the Kouses and Posner model are: Model the way, inspire a shared vision, challenge the process, enable others to act, and encourage the heart (Posner, Crawford & Denniston-Stewart, 2015). Kouses and Posner contend that these five practices are essential elements and practices that leaders should develop and use to ensure success (Kouzes & Posner, 2012; Kouzes & Posner, 2016).

Figure 3. Transformational and Transactional Leadership

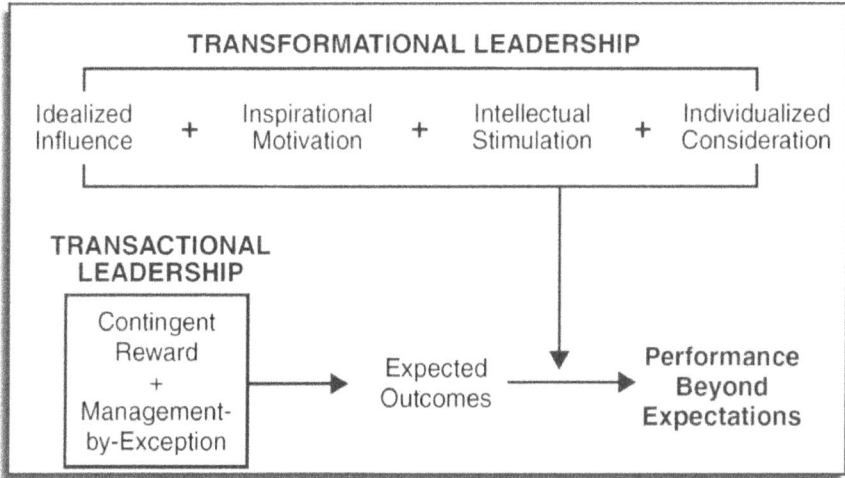

Figure 3. Transformational and Transactional Leadership. Reprinted from *Leadership: Theory and practice* (p. 184), by P. Northouse, 2013, Thousand Oaks, CA: Sage Publications. Copyright 2007 by Sage Publications.

The Five Practices of Exemplary Leadership Model

Model the Way. Leaders establish principles concerning the way people (constituents, peers, colleagues, and customers alike) should be treated and the way goals should be pursued. Standards of excellence are established and then the leaders set the example for others to follow. Because the prospect of complex change can overwhelm people and stifle action, they set interim goals so that people can achieve small wins as they work toward larger objectives. They unravel bureaucracy when it impedes action; they put up signposts when people are unsure of where to go or how to get there; and they create opportunities for victory (Kouzes & Posner, 2012, p. 16).

Inspire a Shared Vision. Leaders passionately believe that they can make a difference. They envision the future, creating an ideal and unique image of what the organization can become. Through their magnetism and quiet persuasion, leaders enlist others in their dreams. They breathe life into their visions and get people to see exciting possibilities for the future (Kouzes & Posner, 2012, p. 17).

Challenge the Process. Leaders search for opportunities to change the status quo. They look for innovative ways to improve the organization. In doing so, they experiment and take risks. And because leaders know that risk taking involves mistakes and failures, they accept the inevitable disappointments as learning opportunities (Kouzes & Posner, 2012, p. 18).

Enable Others to Act. Leaders foster collaboration and build spirited teams. They actively involve others. Leaders understand that mutual respect is what sustains extraordinary efforts; they strive to create an atmosphere of trust and human dignity. They strengthen others, making each person feel capable and powerful (Kouzes & Posner, 2012, p. 20).

Encourage the Heart. Accomplishing extraordinary things in organizations is hard work. To keep hope and determination alive, leaders recognize contributions that individuals make. In every winning team, the members need to share in the rewards of their efforts, so leaders celebrate accomplishments. They make people feel like heroes (Kouzes & Posner, 2012, p. 22).

Figure 4.   Five Practices and Ten Commitments of Exemplary Leadership

The Five Practices of Exemplary Leadership®	Ten Commitments
Model the Way	• Clarify values by finding your voice and affirming shared ideals. • Set the example by aligning actions with shared values.
Inspire a Shared Vision	• Envision the future by imagining exciting and ennobling possibilities. • Enlist others in a common vision by appealing to shared aspirations.
Challenge the Process	• Search for opportunities by seizing the initiative and by looking outward for innovative ways to improve. • Experiment and take risks by constantly generating small wins and learning from experience.
Enable Others to Act	• Foster collaboration by building trust and facilitating relationships. • Strengthen others by increasing self determination and developing competence.
Encourage the Heart	• Recognize contributions by showing appreciation for individual excellence. • Celebrate the values and victories by creating a spirit of community.

Figure 4.   Five Practices and Ten Commitments of Exemplary Leadership. Reprinted from *Leadership challenge* (p. 29), by J. Kouzes & B. Posner, 2012, San Francisco: Jossey-Bass. Copyright 2012 by James M. Kouzes and Barry Z. Posner.

Charismatic Leadership

Charismatic leaders have influenced the history of the world. During the past century there have been both good and bad influential charismatic leaders such as Theodore Roosevelt, Winston Churchill, Adolf Hitler, Benito Mussolini, Fidel Castro, John F. Kennedy, and Barack Obama (Grabo & Van Vugt, 2016; Welch, 2013). There are numerous differences between charismatic leaders which has made it difficult for researchers to identify any agreeable common elements that could predict or identify potential charismatic leadership (Grabo & Van Vugt, 2016).

Charismatic leadership theory is different from other traditional theories in that it is not actually a leadership theory, but rather a characteristic of leadership theory. The use of the term charisma is said to have been created 2000 years ago by St. Paul, who believed that charisma was a heavenly gift (Grabo & Van Vugt, 2016). Max Weber is credited with the formal introduction of transactional leadership in 1947 and introduced the application of the characteristic of charisma within the practice of transactional leadership (Bass, 1997; Winkler, 2010).

The interest in Weber's charismatic research was continued by House (1977) and suggested that there was a connection with a leader's characteristics and behaviors. Self-security, dominance, strong moral conviction, and desire to influence are characteristics of a charismatic leader (House, 1977). Behaviors included empathy and appreciation for followers, and being a role model (Meuser et al., 2016).

While charisma is generally considered a positive characteristic, historical examples like Adolf Hitler show that followers can be influenced. A leader's charisma would be a determinant to their success in crisis emergency situations where followers are driven by the leaders' vision, focus, and direction ((Meuser et al., 2016). The role of followers is critical for the success of a charismatic leader (Meuser et al., 2016).

Servant Leadership

Similar to charismatic leadership, servant leadership is focused more on traits and characteristics than on a defined and accepted leadership theory (Focht & Ponton, 2015). Servant leadership has not been widely accepted nor has there been a unified and agreed upon definition of servant leadership (Neubert, Hunter & Tolentino, 2016). Developed and introduced by Robert Greenleaf in the 1970s, servant leadership was identified by Greenleaf as leaders wanting to help others, a belief that "the servant-leader is servant first" and that the leader serves in a manner that enables followers to be freer, wiser, healthier, more autonomous, and attracts the followers to be servants (Greenleaf, 1970; Liden, Wayne, Chenwei & Meuser, 2014). Greenleaf identified 10 characteristics that servant leaders should be concerned with: (1) listening, (2) empathy, (3) healing, (4) awareness, (5) persuasion, (6) conceptualization, (7) foresight, (8) stewardship, (9) commitment to the growth of people, and (10) building community.

Continuous change in society during the past century resulted in changes in the previously dominant attitudes concerning autocratic and transactional styles of leadership (Avolio, Walumbwa, & Weber, 2009). Greenleaf's approach with servant leadership focused on what was considered a humanistic and relationship approach to followers (Greenleaf, 1970; Liden, Wayne, Chenwei & Meuser, 2014).

The servant leadership concept has a morality point of view that is concerned with the welfare of others and the best interest of followers in mind (Gregoire & Arendt, 2014). Helping followers grow personally and professionally, absence of intimidation, and a safe and encouraging environment were also aspects of Greenleaf's' servant leadership (Gregoire & Arendt, 2014). Servant leaders are driven by their aspiration for helping others (Greenleaf, 1970).

During recent years, executives of corporations in the United States and many corporations have lost their trust rating with the American people (Porter, 2012). Public opinion has shifted towards a position that the executives and corporations are untrustworthy, unethical, and corrupt (Porter, 2012). While servant leadership has yet to be accepted as a mainstream style of leadership, Hesse (2013) learned that characteristics of servant leadership were found in many executive level leaders of companies like Starbucks, San Antonio Spurs, Southwest Airlines, Whole Foods, and Best Buy. These leaders were found to be people and service driven, possess strong values, and were selfless and humble (Hesse, 2013). Huang et al. (2016) found that in the hospitality industry the servant leadership practices of CEOs strongly influenced positive organizational performance and public opinion.

Laissez-faire Leadership

Unlike what is considered traditional leadership practices, laissez-faire leadership is generally defined as a non-transactional and passive avoidant style of leadership (Bass, 1985, 2014; Avolio & Bass, 1991). Laissez-faire is arguably the least studied leadership style due to its absence of traditional leadership behaviors (Sudha, Shahnawaz & Farhat, 2016; Yang, 2015). Laisse-faire leaders are normally absent, detached, and relinquish their responsibilities to subordinates (Bass, 1985; Yang, I. (2015).

Laissez-faire leaders typically do not direct or use authority with their followers, and do not make decision related to day-to-day operations, therefore enabling followers to manage themselves and solve difficulties encountered (Bhatti et al., 2012). Laissez-faire has been found to be less effective in producing operational efficiency when compared with transformational and transactional leadership outcomes (Sudha, Shahnawaz & Farhat, 2016).

Typically, laissez-faire is not a recommended style of leadership, and not suggested in organizational environments where followers do not possess the ability or skills to problem solve, manage, or operate independently (Goodnight, 2011). Although not recommended by a majority of researchers, there are researchers who suggested otherwise (Goodnight, 2011). Leaders may purposely exclude themselves, avoid direct management, and project the appearance of laissez-faire leadership when their intention is to promote empowerment, teamwork, and self-sufficiency (Bhatti et al., 2012; Derue, Nahrgang, Wellman & Humphrey, 2011). Laissez-faire may be considered an appropriate approach in environments where independent thinking and multiple tasks are required by specializations (Goodnight, 2012).

The new century and advancements in technology and globalizations have created new approaches to organizational operations. Remote locations and multiple locations including both home and office has produced a new kind of follower (Wang, 2012). Independent workers from remote work locations requires that they can operate independently without supervision (Sudha, Shahnawaz & Farhat, 2016; Wang, 2012). Leaders of these independent workers may appear in some respects to be laissez-faire practitioners, when in fact they leaders of a new kind of follower capable of performing without traditional leadership practices (Sudha, Shahnawaz & Farhat, 2016; Wang, 2012).

Full-Range Leadership

The previously discussed leadership theories all have a similarity in that each theory, in practice, are independently practiced as a single leadership style. A majority of research in the past, and continue today to focus on single leadership styles and behaviors even though they generally agree that leaders exhibit more than one element of leadership (Bass, 1985; Yukl, 2012). The study of leadership will require further study related to contrasting the various elements of behavior involved in leadership practices (Yukl, 2012).

The full range leadership theory is unique in that it combines elements of transactional, transformation, and laissez-faire leadership into in single model (Sadeghi & Pihie, 2012). The interest in full range leadership has grown over the past several decades and is the highest cited source on leadership (Khan, Ramzan, Ahmed & Nawaz, 2011). Interest in full range leadership is attributed to it embracing a wide range of behavioral traits associated with transactional, transformational, and laisse-faire leadership theories (Zaech & Baldegger, 2017).

Anderson and Sun (2017) suggested that in the past decade traditional leadership theories have started to have overlaps and gaps which identify a need for development of a new full range type of leadership. Advancements in technology, society, and attitudes created a trend for leaders to adapt and utilize multiple elements of various leadership theories such as transactional, transformational, charismatic, and others (Anderson & Sun, 2017).

The full range model (Figure 2) has three components consisting of transactional, transformational, and laisse-faire leadership styles that have a combined nine sub-components or behavior related categories (Avolio, Bass, Jung, 1999). The nine behavior categories are laissez-faire also known as passive avoidance, management by exception (active), management-by-exception (passive), contingent reward, individualized consideration, inspirational motivation, intellectual stimulation, idealized influence-attributes, and idealized influence-behaviors (Mazurkiewicz, 2012; Ravazadeh & Ravazadeh, 2013; Grunewald & Salleh 2013).

Laissez-faire. The first behavior is laisse-faire, also known as passive avoidance and is considered both a leadership style and a category of behavior. Laisse-faire behavior is an absence of leadership, avoidance, and non-involvement with followers (Sudha, Shahnawaz & Farhat, 2016). The Laissez-faire behavior is a method by which leaders pay little or no attention to their subordinates and allow them to perform on their own without supervision (Sudha, Shahnawaz & Farhat, 2016). This method is also considered by some researchers to be a management by exception passive behavior, a behavior that is classified as a category of the transactional style of leadership (Kamisan & King, 2013).

Management by exception (active). The active form of management by exception is a category of transactional leadership and is a method utilized to punish, penalize, or otherwise apply course of action upon subordinates failing to meet tasks or other organizational requirements (Meyer, 2013). This behavior is known for being a straightforward approach with subordinates, confronting them and providing expectations for improvement (Meyer, 2013).

Management-by-exception (passive). The passive approach to management by exception is also a transactional category. The leader that uses this method does address issues similar to active behavior, however, does not confront or directly supervise. The passive leader avoids direct confrontation and waits for situations and errors to occur, and then takes appropriate actions (Northouse, 2013).

Contingent reward. Contingent reward is a fundamental behavior of transactional leadership (Northouse, 2013). The practice of utilizing contingent rewards provides the leader the ability to project power and influence over subordinates while simultaneously empowering subordinates with clear objectives (Northouse, 2013; Robinson & Boies, 2016). Expectations are clear, and subornments receive recognition and rewards for meeting expectations and goals (Robinson & Boies, 2016).

Individual consideration. A significant behavior of transformational leaders is individual consideration. Transformational leaders engage and develop followers by being approachable, personal, and involved in the needs of the followers (Chism & Pang, 2014; Gandolfi, 2012). Transformational behavior enables acceptance of individual differences and encourages acceptance and participation by followers (Kamisan & King, 2013). Transformational behavior engages individuals and serves as a mentor and enabler to establish self-confidence, self-esteem, and focus on individual goals (Calik et al., 2012).

Intellectual stimulation. Transformational leaders are skilled at innovation, creativity, and inspiring others (Boateng, 2012) The transformational leader provides intellectual stimulation through encouraging followers to identify and solve problems, search for opportunities, and empowering them to use their own creativity and vision (Mazurkiewicz, 2012). The transformational leader encourages and enables a continuous learning environment within the organization (Balyer, 2012).

Inspirational motivation. The ability of a leader to utilize inspirational motivational behaviors to create and maintain teams, optimism, enthusiasm, and positive environments within organizations has a positive impact on achieving goals and follower's attitudes (Bass & Avolio, 2004). The goals set by Inspirational leaders are met with enthusiasm and an expectation to succeed, and accomplish organizational requirements (Krishnan, 2012). Inspirational leaders inspire followers to be participants in organizational strategy, planning, and execution (Bass & Avolio, 2004).

Idealized influence (behavioral). The behavior of leaders and the example they set establishes the environment and follower attitudes within organizations (Kouzes & Posner, 2016). Demonstrated ethical conduct accompanied by personal and professional conduct, and clear values provide followers with positive influences and examples to follow (Bass & Avolio, 2004). Leaders applying idealized influence behaviors are perceived by followers as being more proficient and professional (Meyer, 2013).

Idealized influence (attributed). Behavioral versus attributed idealized influence has a distinct difference (Ravazadeh & Ravazadeh, 2013). Behavioral can apply to follower's expectation of conduct and demonstrated conduct by a leader. Attributed encompasses the charismatic influence of a leader, the referent power bestowed on the leader, confidence, respect, and trust of the leader. Followers may emulate the leader who projects attributed idealized influence, perform at a higher level, and seek the leader's approval (Ravazadeh & Ravazadeh, 2013).

The full range leadership model has not surpassed transformational leadership, considered to be the most commonly practiced leadership theory. Full range leadership has identified the practice of leaders combining multiple elements of different leadership theories (Sadeghi & Pihie, 2012). Full range leadership embraces a wide range of behavioral traits associated with transactional, transformational, and laisse-faire leadership theories, and identified a need for further research to compare behavioral elements and conflicting research (Garcia, Duncan, Carmody-Bubb & Ree, 2014; Yukl, 2012).

Figure 5. Full Range Leadership Model

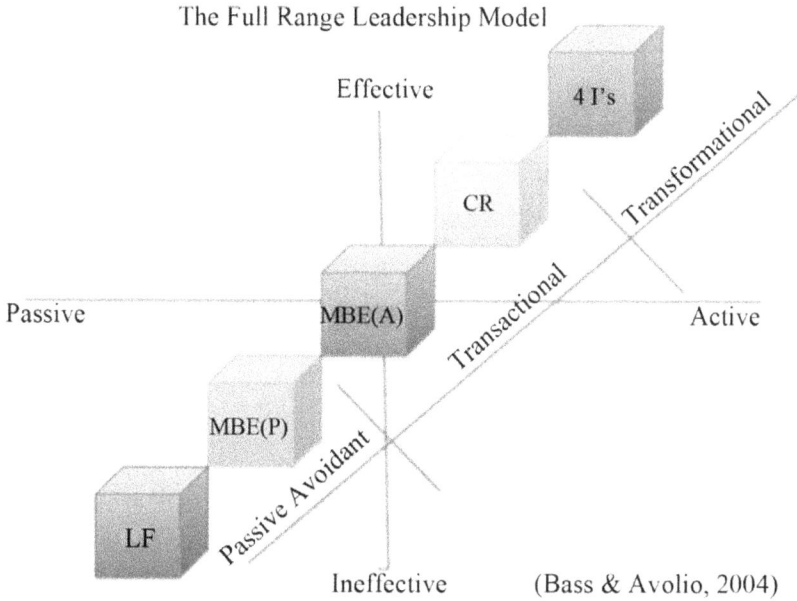

The Full Range Leadership Model

Figure 5. Full Range Leadership Model. Reprinted from "You have what? Personality! Traits that predict leadership styles for elementary principals," by M. Garcia, P. Duncan, M. Carmody-Bubb and M.J. Ree, Psychology, *5*(3), p. 204. Copyright 2014 by the Authors and Scientific Research Publishing Inc.

Adaptive Leadership

The adaptive leadership theory is still in its infancy and considered by many researchers to be contradictory to the premise of traditional leadership theories (Allio, 2013; Latham, 2014). Robert Heifetz is credited with the development of Adaptive leadership, introduced in his 1994 book, "Leadership without Easy Answers" (Haber-Curran & Tillapaugh, 2013; Heifetz, 1994). Transactional, transformation and other traditional leadership theories developed over the decades differ from adaptive leadership theory in that the adaptive leadership approach recognizes a need for requirements beyond the limitations established for individual traditional leadership theories (Heifetz, 1994). Traditional theories impose pre-set practices without options to deviate. The great man theory for example implied that only certain males could be leaders, hence the term "A born leader," whereas adaptive leadership suggested that anyone from any background can be a leader (Allio, 2013; Heifeetz, 1994).

Adaptive leadership is uniquely different from traditional leadership theories. Traditional leadership theory suggested employment of specific behaviors, traits, and other attributes associated with a single theory (Allio, 2013). Adaptive leadership suggested that a leader should be adaptable based on changing situations and events and requires utilizing multiple behaviors and attributes that are elements of more than one traditional leadership theory (Allio, 2013; Heifeetz, 1994).

An argument can be presented that adaptive leadership is no different than full range leadership. Full range leadership theory combines elements of transactional, transformation, and laissez-faire leadership into in single model and therefore applies an adaptive concept where leaders utilize multiple elements of three theories (Sadeghi & Pihie, 2012). The difference between adaptive and full range is that full range is limited to three theories, whereas adaptive suggested that elements from any or all theories can be used by a leader (Allio, 2013; Heifeetz, 1994). Anderson and Sun (2017) suggested that the existing full range theory is outdated and there exists a need for continued research to expand full range leadership to be more accommodating to the expanding needs of society and organizations.

The continual changing global organizational environments has resulted in accelerated advancements in technology and organizational operations (Gu, 2014). The traditional transactional type of leadership practiced in the past is transitioning to a requirement for not just adaptive leaders, but leaders that possess the ability to accept followers' participation in organizational operations and situational changes (Bligh, 2012). Although adaptive leaders must be able to adapt, they must also be capable of focusing on influencing followers to acquire the same adaptive skills and abilities to react to situational change (Bligh, 2012).

One of the many challenges facing all leaders, including adaptive leaders, is the departure of traditional followers, also known as employees, labor, or subordinates (Bligh, 2012; Gu, 2014). The transactional type of follower is a thing of the past and today's followers require leaders who view followers as participants in organizational planning and outcomes (Bligh, 2012; Gu, 2014). Torres and Reeves (2014) suggested that leaders who continue to practice traditional leadership are less successful because they do not envision follower input and needs and lack self-confidence and the ability or desire to adapt. Adaptive leaders should understand and be capable of addressing follower's different needs, perceptions, skills, and approachability (Bligh, 2012).

The complexities of continuous change, transparency, and a more educated and involved base of followers has eliminated the effectiveness of traditional leadership practices (Apenko, & Chernobaeva, 2016). Practitioners of adaptive leadership do not follow traditional routine, but rather develop their own methods and behaviors to quickly adapt to maintain a continual flow of operational efficiency and follower interaction (Brothers, & Schnurman-Crook, 2015; Zimmerly, 2016).

Globalization and continuous advancements have generated a broader awareness of the advanced skills and attributes required of the modern leader (Partida, 2015). Constant change has required leaders to adapt and evolve (Partida, 2015). A result of constant change has created leaders who through their own arrogance, avoidance, and lack of awareness, have failed and ushered in an era of transparency, and follower and stakeholder responsiveness to the requirements for adaptive leadership (Kellerman, 2013). The absence of emotional intelligence, listening, and vision are noted as skills that also contribute to leadership failure (Kaigh et al., 2014).

Future of Leadership

The literature review thus far reviewed multiple leadership theories, each with their own merit and intended application for leadership. Each theory, beginning with the great man theory up to the more recent full range and adaptive theories, have each served or continue to serve the purpose of providing leaders with an established set of designated skills, attributes, and guidelines to effectively lead (Allio, 2013; Sadeghi & Pihie, 2012). The future of leadership theories, their intended applications, their practical applications, and how they will either continue to be utilized or replaced by evolving theories will likely be a continued topic of research (Bennis, 2013; Latham, 2014).

As the world progresses in the twenty-first century, one of the many challenges for organizational leadership is generational differences between the older generation, and the younger generations (Anderson, Baur, Griffith, & Buckley, 2016). The continual growth of the younger generation, commonly referred to as millennials, presents unusual situations, attitudes, and personality differences that impact leadership approaches (Anderson et al., 2016). Millennials adapt to continuous changes in technology and hold a strong advantage over both their older counterparts, and their leaders who often times have difficulties adapting (Kaifi, Nafei, Khanfar, & Kaifi, 2012). Millennials hold varied perspectives related to leadership, teamwork, expectations, and communication, all of which contribute to the challenge for leadership to adapt (Kaifi et al., 2012).

The changing organizational environments impacts the varied business practices, technological changes, stakeholder expectation, while adapting to millennials personality traits (Hartman & McCambridge, 2011). Historically the transition of time from one generation to the next shows changes in values and attitudes (Lyons & Kuron, 2014). Millennials are hard workers and can work well in teams, however they are also more likely to maintain a balanced life and not be inclined to work overtime or weekends (Ferri-Reed, 2012).

The era of organizational memos, paper driven procedures, transactional and authoritarian leadership practices have all but been removed from everyday life (Anderson et al., 2016). The generation of millennials bring their own technological advantages to an organization. Unlike many of their older generational counterparts, millennials grow up with email, texting, and other technologies as a normal part of their lives. Technological change is not something millennials have to adapt to (Hartman & McCambridge, 2011; Piper, 2012).

Due in part to social and technological exposure of millennials, adaptability to change can be considered a second nature attribute (Stewart, Oliver, Cravens & Oishi, 2016). The older generational followers and leaders can find it difficult to adapt and embrace the continual changes in organizational advancements (Stewart et al., 2016). The millennial generation may be subject to less independence, short attention span, and a tendency for instant gratification, all of which can be a negative trait for future leaders (Clark, 2017).

Changing societal attitudes towards organizational success or failure has produced the desired trait of emotional intelligence for both older and younger generations of leaders and followers (Doe, Ndinguri & Phipps, 2015). There has been debate concerning emotional intelligence and if possession of it is something learned or an innate trait (Tyler, 2015). Regardless of the source of emotional intelligence, it has become a desired quality for modern leaders (Tyler, 2015). The skill and ability for a leader to emotionally gage the human factor related to organizational performance has become an important trait for a leader (Dabke, 2016). The success and public perception of an organizational is believed to be attributed to the emotional intelligence qualities of both the leader and followers, and in many instances positive and productive working environments is a result of the emotional intelligence practices within as organizations (Dabke, 2016).

Transparency is another challenge for organizational leaders. The era of social media, technological progress, and corporate responsibility has created an expectation for transparency by stakeholders and the public related to organizational affairs (Bennis, 2013). During the past several decades, bank scandals, Wiki Leaks, and other ethical related scandals lead the way for the demand for more transparency (Press & Arnould, 2014).

Transparency produces a positive effect on followers' performance (Farrell, 2016). The transparent organizational environment increases followers drive, sense of participation, and awareness of recognition (Farrell, 2016). Transparency generates increased organizational efficiency resulting in an improved benefit for followers, organization, and stakeholders (Farrell, 2016).

In past decades, the issue of financial reporting has been a concern for all organizations in all industries and government agencies. Historically organizations had a reputation for only reporting positive financial information, or falsifying information (Kundeliene & Leitoniene, 2015). The evolution of technology, speed of communication, and social media have created an environment of timely awareness of operations and any pressing issue that may arise (Kundeliene & Leitoniene, 2015). These changes contributed to environments of forced transparency within organizations, and the requirement for leaders to adapt to function in transparent environments (Kundeliene & Leitoniene, 2015; Press & Arnould, 2014).

The term "E-Leadership" was introduced just over a decade ago and has since become a commonly used term (Avolio, Sosik, Kahai, & Baker, 2014). The evolution of technology and continuous change in communications and various other business operations has resulted in an additional requirement for leaders to be adaptable to e-leadership methods (Avolio et al., 2014). In addition to traditional leadership concerns associated with past practices, today's leaders must take into account multi-cultural considerations, globalization, time, and distance (Lilian, 2014). The advent of virtual teams has resulted in improved team member communication and collaboration, while allowing the leaders flexibility to delegate and empower followers (Cowan, 2014). Virtual team effectiveness is improved through established communication methods and review processes that incorporate team member contributions with leader's oversight and review (Morgan, Paucar-Caceres, & Wright, 2014).

Globalization and advancements in multiple organizational operating systems has presented additional challenges for leaders (Lilian, 2014). Organizations have transitioned through restructuring and adoption of new ways to conduct business (Lilian, 2014). The evolution of remote and geographically separated work forces has influenced the development of virtual teams (Avolio et al., 2014). The virtual team concept presents challenges for leaders to operate across multiple time zones without physical face-to-face contact or interaction (Lilian, 2014). These leaders must adapt to delegation and trust in followers, and in their own confidence and security with the knowledge that followers will produce desired results (Savolainen, 2014).

Information security is another challenge facing leaders. Advancements in technological security have created additional opportunities for theft of intellectual property and employee and customer personal data (Sabnis & Charles, 2012). Changes to government laws and policies, in addition to continuous software advancements, dictate constant preventive measures related to information security (Harvey & Harvey, 2014). Organizational leaders are faced with maintaining their personal knowledge awareness and staying up to date with technology and security advancements and prevention (Harvey & Harvey, 2014).

The future of leadership is faced with dual challenges related to women in leadership roles. A history of male cultured dominated leadership in society and the prejudicial stereotype attitudes towards women are two barriers that restrict women's advancements to upper-level leadership roles (Moreno & McLean, 2016; Sindell & Shamberger, 2016). The great man theory of leadership and the term itself reflected a societal perception and attitude that leadership was a men only position (Cawthon, 1996). The inclusion of women in upper-level leadership roles in recent years has increased, however still lags in equality and stereotypical associations with women (Hoyt & Murphy, 2016). One example of the stereotypes regarding women in leadership is the "women take care" and "men take charge" attitudes (Hoyt & Murphy, 2016).

It is estimated that as of 2015 women accounted for only 24 percent of executive vice-president level type positions (Sindell & Shamberger, 2016). The number of women university presidents is estimated to be 26 percent (DeFrank-Cole, Latimer, Neidermeyer, & Wheatly, 2016). The success and advancing social acceptance of women on equal status is in part attributed to overcoming generational bias, and the millennial attitudes of equal gender equality (DeFrank-Cole, Latimer, Neidermeyer, & Wheatly, 2016). Global views concerning women as leaders can be an added obstacle for women advancing to leadership roles (McLean & Beigi, 2016). The variety of national, ethnic, and regional cultures, combined with religious beliefs and traditions, impose limitations on the acceptance of women in leadership roles (McLean & Beigi, 2016).

Future leader's faces multiple challenges associated with the millennial workforce, emotional intelligence, security, e-leadership, virtual work environments, globalization, and the role of women (Avolio et al., 2009). Leaders practicing existing leadership theory are confronted with utilizing outdated theories developed prior to current changes in society and advancements in technology and globalization (Bennis, 2013; Latham, 2014). The practice of existing leadership theories does not allow for adaptation to change, and therefore limits leader's courses of action (Torres & Reeves, 2014).

The development of the full range leadership theory combined transformation, transactional, and laisse-faire, and is an example of changing theory to adapt, however full range theory is limited to elements of the three theories (Sadeghi & Pihie, 2012). Full range theory is not a newly developed theory, but simply a merging of theories that were not developed for today's challenges and advancements (Latham, 2014; Yukl, 2012

The leadership theories previously discussed are summarized in figure 6 below.

Figure 6. Leadership Theories

Theory	Description
Great Man	Introduced in the 1840s by Thomas Carlyle. Belief that leaders were born and not made and that leaders are exceptional people, born with innate qualities, destined to lead (Bass & Bass, 2008; Hoffman et al., 2011).
Trait	Belief that personal traits determine, in part, a leader's ability to lead. Trait theorists believed that individuals were born with certain leadership traits and that these traits could not be learned nor gained through education or training (Northouse, 2013).
Behavioral	Belief that behavior drives the leaders' performance. Refinement of the situational viewpoint and focuses on identifying the situational variables that can predict appropriate response to situations (Gupta & Singh, 2013).
Contingency	Developed in 1967 by Fiedler and theorized that specific situations would dictate which type of response and leadership was required to address the

	situation with a successful reaction (Fiedler, 1967; Prindle, 2012).
Situational	Developed in the 1960s by Blanchard based on a concept that different situations would require varying responses. The theory suggested that leaders had to adapt their leadership approach based on the level of individual follower development (Blanchard & Hersey, 1996; Northouse, 2013).
Authoritarian	Also known as autocratic, was introduced in Iowa studied by Lewin, Lippitt, and White in 1938. Autocratic is characterized by individual control over all situations and is a method utilized by leaders to dictate, tell, or demand their subordinates to perform tasks (Elqadri et al., 2015; Flynn, 2015).
Path-Goal	Path-Goal leadership is based on House (1996) theory that followers are provided goals through value rewards, and the leaders provide the best method, or path, to accomplish the goals. An element of path-goal theory is the premise that leaders should increase the motivation, satisfaction, and performance of followers through

	communicating, rewarding, and eliminating obstacles that could interfere with accomplishing the goals (Hollenbeck, DeRue & Nahrgang, 2015; House, 1996).
Transactional	Developed in 1947 by Max Weber and based on management by exception, contingent reward, and goal achievement. Transactional is a method of exchanging behaviors by leaders and followers that generate rewards. A transactional leader gains performance of followers through contingent rewarding (Bass, 1997; Humphrey, 2013).
Transformational	Developed by James MacGregor in the 1970s Transformational leadership is defined as a method where leaders in a sense transformed themselves, and through changes in their behaviors and actions connected and interacted with their followers creating higher levels of motivation, morality and ultimately performance outcomes (Allio, 2013; Northouse, 2013).
Charismatic	1948 Max Weber introduced the application of the characteristic of charisma within the practice of

	transactional leadership. Self-security, dominance, strong moral conviction, and desire to influence are characteristics of a charismatic leader (House, 1977; Winkler, 2010).
Servant	Developed in the 1970s by Robert Greenleaf. Servant leadership concept is to have a moral position that ensures well-being of followers and leaders should lead with best interest for followers (Greenleaf, (1977).
Laissez-Faire	The concept was introduced in Iowa studied by Lewin, Lippitt, and White in 1938. Laissez-faire is a non-transactional and passive avoidant style of leadership. Laisse-faire leaders are normally absent, detached, and relinquish their responsibilities to subordinates (Avolio & Bass, 1991; Bass, 1985).
Full Range	Developed in the 1980s and 1990s by Bass and Avolio. Full range leadership combines elements of transactional, transformation, and laissez-faire leadership theories into in single model (Sadeghi & Pihie, 2012).

Adaptive	Developed by Robert Heifetz in the 1990s. Adaptive leadership suggested that a leader should be adaptable based on changing situations and events and requires utilizing multiple behaviors and attributes that are elements of more than one traditional leadership theory (Allio, 2013; Heifetz, 1994).

Continual Change and Transparency

The study of leadership has experienced unprecedented growth in the past twenty years providing a multitude of models and suggested methods for ideal leadership (Allio, 2013). Internet searches on sites like Amazon provide an estimated 60,000 results for books and 80,000 results for leadership, and millions of results on Google (Allio, 2013). The vast number of studies and other leadership related resources has provided both a base for study, but also a field for conflicting arguments relating to change and transparency (Allio, 2013; Dew et al., 2011). The phenomenon of continual changing and transparent organizational environments has emerged in recent years and will continue to do so in the future (Dew et al., 2011; Torres & Reeves, 2013).

Before his death in 2014, the renowned pioneer in the field of leadership, Warren Bennis, believed that leadership had been fundamentally changed due to globalization, technology, and digitization. The suggestion by Bennis has been echoed by other researchers who have identified the phenomenon of an evolving and constant progress within society affecting all aspects of global interaction, economics, business, and organizational environments (Dew et al., 2011; Torres & Reeves, 2013). Unlike other disciplines, leadership studies have not been restricted and has been researched and applied across multiple disciplines such as management, social sciences, political sciences, psychology, and all organizational structures regardless of specialization (Eberly, Johnson, Hernandez, & Avolio, 2013). Bennis (2013) suggested that these types of changes and applications created a world of continual change and an almost instant transparent operating environment that made leadership more difficult.

The advancements of technology and social media have generated an ability for instant transparency of information within organizations and an increased necessity for leaders to possess an ability to multi-task and adapt to change (Bennis, 2013; Torres & Reeves, 2013). A survey of 547 participants showed that along with constant change in a variety of industries, organizational leadership was required to evolve to maintain pace (Partida, 2015). The continual changes in operating trends and globalization resulted in a more awareness of leadership requirements and approach to organizational leadership (Partida, 2015).

Fibuch (2011) discussed how change during the past 20 years in organizational structures has impacted the effectiveness of leadership. The manner in which organizations are run, the technologies supporting them, demands by stakeholders for access, and regulatory changes have resulted in the way leaders lead their organizations (Fibuch, 2011). The increased complexities of organizational leadership have generated a pattern of leadership failures, characterized by leader's lack of self-awareness, arrogance, ignoring warning signs, and avoidance of personal responsibility for organizational shortfalls (Fibuch, 2011). Due in part to these changes leaders are becoming less important and more vulnerable to stakeholder and follower influence and power, and transparency (Kellerman, 2013).

Trust is another factor that has influence on transparency (Auger, 2014). Leadership and organizational transparency not only aid in the development of trust with stakeholders, but projects an image of an organization's credibility, legitimacy, and authenticity (Auger, 2014). The 2015 Edelman Trust Barometer reported that CEOs were not trusted as credible representatives of their organizations and had trust levels of 43 percent compared to industry experts, technical professionals, and academics (Edelman, 2015). The Edelman report results estimated that 70 percent of participants had a negative perception of CEOs trustworthiness, a factor that contributes to lack of transparency.

A values survey of 50 participants by Marque (2010) suggested that in the era of the new millennium followers have transitioned from a focus on financial and material gain toward a desire to be more relationship and values driven within their work environment. The survey demonstrates a change in society's perceptions of what is important to individuals at their workplace, and the importance of leaders possessing skills at adapting to these changes (Marques, 2010; Roof, 2015). Various studies of followers suggested that just like all leaders can be different, so too are followers in their needs, and their perceptions of leaders (Bligh, 2012). Leaders' interaction and understanding of the varied differences in followers is another challenge facing leaders that requires adaptive skills (Bligh, 2012).

There are countless leadership theories, models, courses, books, and other leadership related material, and yet none of these have improved or identified a best type of leader (Allio, 2013; Kellerman, 2013). The continued trend of leadership study has ignored the advancements in follower involvement within industries and failed to recognize that followers have become experts, make decisions, and perform their jobs without direct leadership (Kellerman, 2013). Eisenbeiss (2015) suggested that the mindset of followers is transitioning towards a more moral, ethical, and satisfaction standpoint, requiring their leaders to not only possess the same views, but to be active practitioners of those beliefs.

Torres and Reeves (2013) suggested that changes within traditional organizational practices have generated new requirements and approaches in leadership. It is not enough for an organization's leadership to have the ability to adapt to change; the business itself must operate in a manner where its employees and structure is capable of adapting to constant challenges (Rietsema & Watkins, 2012). Shifts in business practices related to uncertainty, inter-dependent and multi-company structures, pervasiveness of business technology, social responsibility, lack of trust, and diverse competition have created the need for leaders to possess adaptive skill traits (Torres & Reeves, 2013).

Kaigh et al., (2014) suggested that a gap exists between leadership hard and soft skills, where traditional structured leadership styles are inadequately supported by the soft skills of vision, listening, and emotional intelligence. Research suggested that leaders who exhibit low levels of interaction and emotional intelligence with followers are less effective and acquire lower follower loyalty (Stoker, Grutterink, & Kolk, 2012). Research gathered from 38 top management teams (TMT) and their respective CEOs revealed that in cases where low levels of feedback was desired, the effectiveness and performance was positively impacted in organizational change by transformational CEOs (Stoker, Grutterink, & Kolk, 2012).

The uncertainty of organizational environments in all industries has created the need for leadership throughout all levels of organizational structure to adapt independently and collectively to ensure goals are achieved (Torres & Reeves, 2013). Dew et al., (2011) cited an example of a $26 billion budget reduction in California in 2006 applied retroactively and caused negative economic impact on the state, its employees, and government agencies. This example demonstrated the need for leaders to possess the skill to be adaptive and make effective long-term decisions instead of making decisions based on a reactionary impulse to make short-term fixes to situations (Dew et al., 2011).

Rietsema and Watkins (2012) indicated that leaders and their organizations are only part of an overall issue, and that leadership should recognize and accept a world where the global business environment is in a state of constant change. The complexities of global logistics and evolving business models inhibit many leaders from successful performance due to a combination of organizational structure and self-imposed limitations on the part of leadership (Rietsema & Watkins, 2012). A review of ten top-tier academic journals showed an increase in leadership research related to changes in leadership practices since the turn of the millennium (Dinh, 2014).

The research suggested that there is an ever-increasing awareness of traits, ethics, and morals requirements of leaders that identify with followers and stakeholders' interest (Dinh, 2014).

Adapting to changing technologies and employing the changes is one aspect of a leaders' ability to use enhanced traits and capacities to leverage increasing shareholder involvement in organizational affairs (Bennis, 2013; Hartnell et al., 2016). Current and future leaders in all industries will have to maintain up to date proficiency in technology advancements and social media management, as well as focus, adapt to change, and be capable of managing change in order to lead the diverse organizational environment (Bennis, 2013).

Conflicting and Outdated Theories

There are conflicting views concerning transformational, transactional, and other leadership styles, their applications, and the overall study of leadership (Latham, 2014). Research by Qu (2015) suggested that although transformational leadership is supposed to drive positive follower performance, the study produced conflicting data suggesting that transformational leadership suppressed creativity and follower engagement (Qu, Janssen, & Shi, 2015). DeRue (2011) suggested that the study of leadership is engrained with limited and conflicting practices that confuse leadership with supervision and ignore the ever-growing requirements and complexities of leadership at the organizational level. DeRue (2011) further suggested that while scholars of leadership theory have been focused on more visible and scientific advancements, they have not focused on collective and other attributes beyond the individual leader and have disregarded the expanding requirements for modern leaders. Kaigh et al. (2014)

discussed the changes taking place within organizational operations and how leaders are transitioning to what is described as a dynamic approach to leadership.

Traditional leadership has historically been driven by so called hard skills such as cost controls, competition, and analytical thinking, however the soft skills of listening, collaboration, knowledge sharing and others have become a necessary requirement for today's organizational success (Kaigh et al., 2014). McCleskey (2014) suggested that it has been difficult to identify specific behavioral theories or a specific leadership style that is entirely effective, and even suggested that there is not a single effective leadership style. Silva (2014) suggested that there are conflicting perceptions and viewpoints regarding leadership by academia, academic researchers, and organizations where leadership is practiced. Van Dierendonck (2011) suggested that there exist extensive similarity and overlap within leadership styles, however many researchers treat each as independent and different.

The continued growth of multiple environmental factors within modern organizations has resulted in increased difficulty of leadership to be effective (Latham, 2014). Latham (2014) suggested that transformational leadership lacks a complete solution to leadership and encourages a so called "ends justify the means" application. Ling et al., (2008) argued that transformational CEOs are more likely to produce higher organizational performance relating to stakeholder engagement and productivity than counterparts who practice other leadership styles or possess lower levels of transformational traits. The emergence of servant and spiritual leadership theories, which focus more towards leader engagement with followers, also conflict with elements of transformational and transactional theories and have created wider conflicting views concerning effective leadership styles (Latham, 2014).

McCleskey (2014) discussed criticisms of transformational, transactional, and situational leadership styles. Transformation leadership lacks significant research that provides specific outcomes on situational responses and an ability to adapt to change, while transactional leadership lacks qualities to generate long-term relationship and is resistant to adaptability or reaction to situational changes (McCleskey, 2014). Situational leadership is criticized for lacking consistency and is viewed as being open to interpretation and contradictions which make it difficult to identify specific elements (McCleskey, 2014).

Ling et al., (2008) explored the effect that transformational CEO's have on organizational performance and suggested that the attributes and traits demonstrated by transformational leaders and positive influences are observed and imitated by subordinates, resulting in higher level of organizational performance. Transformational leaders also possess the skills and traits to adapt and overcome changing environments that inhibit organizational performance (Ling et al., 2008). Silva (2014) suggested that leaders must possess certain traits such as virtue, charisma, or style over employees to be effective, however conflicting research and leaders own perspectives suggested otherwise and indicate that leadership may not be dictated by a prescribed set of standards. Latham (2014) discussed the historical research of leadership and suggested the need to move away from the predominant quantitative approach and focus towards qualitative or consortium type of research to identify what methods, traits, or styles are effective.

Trait Approach to Leadership

There has been disagreement concerning the trait approach to leadership versus a style approach (Northouse, 2013). Proponents of the trait approach such as Northouse (2013) argued that it is traits of a leader that distinguish the type of style a leader practices and determines the effectiveness of a leader. Bennett (2009) conducted a study in which transactional and transformational leadership were compared and found that transformational leaders had a stronger effect on subordinate performance. Kovjanic, Schuh, Jonas, Quaquebeke, and Dick (2012) explored transformational leadership further and suggested that the traits of transformational leaders impacted follower fulfillment and leadership success. Sadeghi and Pilhie (2012) research supports the concept that transformational leaders use of traits such as inspirational, influential and follower consideration were predictors of success.

Ardichvili and Manderscheid (2008) discussed both sides of the argument and the viewpoint that style is prominent, and traits have little impact on leadership style. Bennis (2013) and Northouse (2013) suggested that traits are what define leaders' abilities to lead, and Northouse identifies intelligence, self-confidence, determination, integrity, and sociability as five major leadership traits. Northouse identifies intelligence to be reasoning ability, and self-confidence is the ability of a leader to have confidence in their own skills and competencies (Northouse, 2013). Determination is demonstrating persistence and personal drive to accomplish a task (Northouse,

2013). Integrity is a trait of possessing trustworthiness and honesty, and sociability is the leader's ability to establish a rapport of being approachable and someone who can interact on a personal and social level with others (Northouse, 2013).

Rietsema and Watkins (2012) suggested that confidence is an important leadership trait and one that most CEO's lack. Rietsema and Watkins (2012) suggested that CEOs doubted their own ability to cope with the complexity of changing operational environments, and over half lacked the confidence to manage effectively when faced with the shifting business. Rietsema and Watkins (2012) conducted interviews with C-suite executives and groups of consultants from three different industries and found that these individuals each had similar doubts about their own ability to lead and manage in their respective responsibilities.

The trait of experience provides added insight into trait performance (Sarros & Sarros, 2011). The differences between experienced and inexperienced leadership in relationship to leadership and initiatives were explored using mixed method research (Sarros & Sarros, 2011). Mission-centered, performance-centered, and culture-centered leadership performance were examined, and the results concluded that with experience and added intellectual stimulation, leaders would produce higher outcomes (Sarros & Sarros, 2011). Experience aids in adding a level of confidence to a leader and contributes to the overall leaders' effectiveness and attaining outcomes (Sarros & Sarros, 2011).

Rietsema and Watkins (2012) suggested that leaders fail to understand and recognize the depth and intricacies of their respective industries and concluded that the portrayal of current leadership is an inability to operate in the growing advancement of organizational environments and lack the traits needed to function effectively. Ethics of leaders is another trait directly influenced by leaders (Groves & LaRocca, 2011). Groves and LaRocca (2011) analyzed the relationship of leadership performance and stakeholder values and expectations, identifying a link between stakeholder values, expectations, and implied expectations of leadership. Mixed method research and split-sample methodology were used to test data from 122 leaders and 458 of their subordinates producing several outcomes relating to each of their studies. The findings showed that leaders' ethical values (Kantian principles) were associated with follower ratings of transformational leadership. Leaders with teleological ethical values (utilitarianism) were associated with follower ratings of transactional leadership, and showed a direct relationship between leadership and ethics, and that ethical expectations influence leadership and follower performance (Groves & LaRocca, 2011).

Changing organizational structures and pre-set expectations may also be a factor in leaders failing to adapt to trends and advancements in organizational environments (Rietsema & Watkins, 2012). Andressen, Konradt, and Neck (2012) presented the definition of self-leadership as a process to improve motivation and influence self-direction and defined transformational leadership as having four dimensions: idealized influence, inspirational motivation, intellectual stimulation, and individualized considerations. Andressen et al., (2012) also added that transformational leadership is a process for inspiring subordinates to collectively share the vision of the leader and motivate others to go beyond their individual interest and be a team player. The findings suggested that transformational leaders possess motivation and self-leadership traits (Andressen et al., 2012).

Summary

The literature review discussed a brief history of leadership, leadership theory, the future of leadership, and the sub-themes of continual change and transparency, conflicting and outdated theories, and trait approach to leadership. The literature reviewed 177 sources obtained from scholarly peer-reviewed articles, journals, and books utilizing EBSCO Host™, ProQuest™, Google Scholar™ and Northcentral University library databases.

The literature reviewed the history of leadership research and theory, beginning with the great man theory and progressing through path-goal, transactional, transformational, and various other theories researched during the past century (Bennis, 2013; Allio, 2013). The phenomenon of continually changing environments within organizations and society was reviewed, followed by review of conflicting and outdated research concerning leadership theory and style (Dew et al., 2011; Torres & Reeves, 2011). Finally, the trait approach to leadership and traits related to leadership was reviewed (Northouse, 2013; Sadeghi, 2012). The literature identified for this review supports the premise of a continually changing organizational environment, conflicting leadership theories, and trait approach to leadership.

CHAPTER 3

RESEARCH METHOD

The changing organizational environments of the 21st century have resulted in a problem with the continued use of outdated leadership theories (Bennis, 2013; Latham, 2014). Contrary to the teachings of academics, numerous leaders no longer practice traditional leadership styles and have transitioned towards enhanced approaches including practicing several leadership styles simultaneously (Dinh, et al., 2014; Kaigh, et al., 2014; Srinivasan, 2010). According to Torres and Reeves (2014) and Sarros and Sarros (2011), leaders continuing to practice traditional leadership are less effective due to a lack of confidence, lack of adaptive capacity skills, and other factors. A review of the general problem, specific problem, purpose, and research method and design will be reviewed in remainder of this chapter.

The general problem was the emergence of continual changing 21st century organizational environments combined with the practice of traditional leadership theories and styles, that were not designed to address 21st century organizational issues associated with technology, globalization, and transparency, produce fewer effective leaders (Bennis, 2013; Latham, 2014; Rietsema & Watkins, 2012).

According to McCleskey (2014) and Silva (2014), there is not a single effective leadership style, and there are conflicting perceptions and viewpoints regarding leadership by academia, academic researchers, and organizations where leadership is practiced.

The specific problem was a lack of understanding of why organizational leaders have transitioned from academically recommended leadership theories to their own non-traditional leadership practices. The conflicting perceptions and leadership practices noted in the general problems overlaps into the specific problem and produces a gap between recommended practice and actual practice by leaders (Dinh, et al., 2014; Kaigh, et al., 2014). The practice by leaders of merging multiple leadership theories into a single leadership practice has yet to be identified or associated with a leadership theory or model (Dinh, et al., 2014; Kaigh, et al., 2014).

The purpose of this phenomenological qualitative study was to explore why organizational leaders have transitioned from academically recommended leadership theories to their own non-traditional leadership practices. Participant interviews will provide data explaining why they ignored existing recommended leadership theory and what specifics, be it technological changes, organizational transparency, globalization, or other issues caused them to transition to their own non-traditional leadership practice. The data obtained from the study supported and contributed to Bennis (2013) and Latham's (2014) belief that there exists, a need to identify and study emerging theory relating to non-traditional leadership practices and identify theories that are no longer relevant or meet the originally envisioned goals.

The Creswell (2014) structured and semi-structured participant interview format was utilized for this study and is the most suitable method for gathering research data. Marshall, Cardon, Poddar, and Fontenot (2013) suggested that there is not a set or agreed upon sample size for qualitative research; however, they do cite several recommended sample-sizing guidelines including that of Creswell (2014) who suggested 10-20 participants for a qualitative study. An estimated 20 participants were scheduled for interviews and upon interviewing the first 13 participants, it was determined that additional data would not change the outcome of the research questions, and data saturation was satisfied (O'Reilly & Parker, 2013).

Research Design

A phenomenological qualitative research methodology was utilized for this study. Personal interviews with study participants were used to collect data and a combination of direct and open-ended questions were asked of participants. The design utilized unstructured and semi-structured interviews which were transcribed using MAXQDA data analysis software. Data was identified, coded, and aligned with research questions (Marshall, et al. (2013).

The purpose for utilizing personal interviews was to explore the associated lived experiences and rationale of the participants for their choices of leadership practices. The use of qualitative research is defined as a focus on people in their natural settings and describing their settings in their own words (Creswell, 2012; Edmonds & Kennedy, 2017). Qualitative research also addresses either the creating or generating of new theory or hypotheses, achieving an understanding of the issues, or developing detailed stories to describe a phenomenon (Creswell, 2014; Yates & Leggett, 2016). This research study did not require experimentation and given that the research topic was more related to behavior practiced by individual leaders than measurable numeric or statistical research, Edmonds and Kennedy (2017) suggested that the qualitative method of research is more appropriate for this type of research.

Population

Research data was obtained from participants from multiple geographic locations and industries within the United States. The participants were individuals personally and professionally known to this researcher, and from professional social media connections on LinkedIn. The screening criteria required that participants possessed 20 or more years of leadership experience, and that their most recent experience was at the executive level equivalent to the CEO, Vice President, or Director positions, and that military participants were at Lieutenant Colonel through General Officer ranks, and enlisted participants were at the E-8 or E-9 ranks. Bias was avoided by means of asking questions that were not leading and did not mention specific leadership theory. The questions were structured in a manner to identify trait behaviors and allow participants to provide their own perceptions, feelings, and practices without associating responses to specific leadership theory.

Sample

An aspect of qualitative research is that it is subjective, and the researcher can view the topic with personal interest while providing opportunity to listen, observe, and interpret findings (Donnelly, 2017). Participants were recruited from a combination of personal and professional friendships and connections of this researcher, and from professional social media connections on LinkedIn. Researchers' personal and professional experiences can add a level of subject matter expertise to a topic (Anfara & Mertz, 2015; Creswell, 2014). This researcher' own personal and professional experiences with both civilian and military organizations will add a level of subject matter expertise in leadership and with the interpretation of participants' information.

The recommended 10 to 20 participants suggested by Creswell (2014) provided enough data to determine categories, themes, and information as suggested by Marshall, et al. (2013) to characterize the phenomenon being studied. The interview participants were experienced leaders across multiple industries at their place of employment worldwide employed in modern digital and transparent organizational environments. There were 13 participants interviewed for this study. O'Reilly and Parker (2013) recommend that after interviewing the initial first 10 participants, if it is determined that additional data will not change the outcome of the research questions, data saturation would be satisfied.

Materials/Instrumentation

Unstructured and semi-structured interviews were the primary tools used to collect data from "C" suite executives and other participants with over 20 years of leadership experience and was available by means of this researcher's personal connections. The interviews were conducted in person face to face or use of video chat technology. Audio recording and a dissertation transcription service was utilized to transcribe the interviews. Member checking was validated by returning transcripts of interviews to participants to review for accuracy.

Interviews allow for open-ended type questions and are not guided nor structured in a manner to solicit a specific answer (Edmonds & Kennedy, 2017). The interview process is used to solicit participants' own interpretations of experiences (Edmonds & Kennedy, 2017). Anfara and Mertz (2015) suggested that interview conversations can be used to develop interpretations of information collected from participants' contributions to a study and be used to confirm and support findings.

Data Collection and Analysis

Prior to the start of research, an application was submitted for approval by the IRB of Northcentral University (IRB). This study focused on the personal lived experiences and perspectives of participant's leadership practices, and the rational for those practices. The process of collecting data began with emails and personal contact to potential participants to solicit their participation in the study. The primary tools that were utilized for this study were the unstructured and semi-structured interview. These tools were selected because they are the recommended method for data collection in qualitative studies (Creswell, 2014; Marshall et al., 2013). The purpose of the study and the interview process was provided to participants and reviewed (Appendix A), as was the informed consent (Appendix B). The data collection was obtained by the use of the semi-structured interview utilizing open-ended questions (Appendix C).

Participants agreeing to participate and who had 20 plus years of leadership experience were asked to agree to an approximate thirty-minute interview to be conducted either in person, or by use of video chat technology. Interviews were transcribed using MAXQDA data analysis software. Themes, phrases, keywords and any parallels found in the interview transcripts were identified, coded, and aligned with research questions (Marshall, et al. (2013). Confidentiality and anonymity was, and will be maintained by use of numeric identifiers for each participant (Marshall, et al. (2013). The researcher will keep the names and associated codes locked in his home office desk drawer. The recordings and transcripts will also be kept in the locked home office desk drawer. Any electronic versions of transcripts will be kept in a password protect folder on a flash drive which will be kept in a locked drawer in the researcher's home office. Participants were provided transcripts of their interviews for review to ensure reliability, trustworthiness, and to satisfy member check.

Assumptions

There was an expectation of honesty by the participants and that they possess the experience to provide accurate responses with rational explanations for their choices in their respective leadership styles and traits practiced. There was an assumption that this researcher would identify and recruit between 10 and 20 qualified participants possessing 20 plus years of executive level leadership experience. During the recruitment process of participants, there may be barriers to accessing the participants, such as scheduling conflicts, accessibility, or unwillingness to participate.

Limitations

Potential participants for the study comprise of individuals from multiple geographic locations and can limit accessibility. The recommended requirement by Creswell (2014) of 10 to 20 participants may cause an inability to recruit the required participants for the study. Data collected from participants was based on their personal perspectives and practices without any quantitative research or statistical data to support the findings. There is numerous research on the subject of leadership, however there is limited research on the topic of leaders transitioning from traditional leadership practices towards non-traditional methods.

Delimitations

This study was conducted utilizing a limited or narrow range of participants with specific requirements. Given the 20 plus years of experience requirement, this restricts the age of participants to individuals who were over 40 years old, and therefore eliminating perspectives of younger aged individuals. This study focused only on the leader perspective and not the followers.

Ethical Assurances

Data was not collected until the IRB approved the study. Identify of the participants is confidential and not identified in the study materials or text. Participant privacy was protected. Honesty, collection of accurate data, and high standards were observed for the study.

An e-mail of introduction (Appendix A) was sent to potential participants. Upon a participant's acceptance to participate, an e-mail (Appendix B) with an informed consent form was forwarded to the participants. The content of the emails provided details of how data would be confidential and how the interview would be conducted.

Participation in this study was voluntary and participants were provided the option to withdraw from the study at any time.

Participants were provided information in the email and informed consent that they were able to utilize to determine if they wanted to volunteer for the study. The participants were given a transcript of the interview and given an opportunity to confirm its content. All data collected during the study was stored in password-protected files, on a flash drive which will be kept in a locked desk drawer.

Summary

The purpose of this qualitative study was to explore and collect data regarding organizational leaders and their decision to ignore academically recommended leadership theory, and why they transition to practicing their own modified non-traditional leadership style, a practice not yet associated with a leadership theory or model. This study collected data that can be utilized to conduct further research on the topic of evolving leadership and the transition from traditional leadership theory practices.

Requirements for the study were reviewed in the chapter including the restatement of the general problem, specific problem, and purpose of the study. The Creswell (2014) structured and semi-structured interview format was identified as the primary research tool, and 10-20 participants was identified as a recommended sample size. The population and sample for the study was identified as participants possessing 20 or more years of leadership experience and recruited from multiple geographic locations. A total of 13 participants were interviewed for this study. Ethical standards and participant's privacy was reviewed and were maintained.

LEADERSHIP

CHAPTER 4

FINDINGS

The purpose of this phenomenological qualitative study was to evaluate lived experiences and explore why organizational leaders transitioned from academically recommended leadership theories to their own non-traditional leadership practices. The premise for this research was based on a combination of literature by Allio (2013), Bennis (2013), Derue and Wellman (2009), Latham (2014), Marshall, et al. (2013), Northouse (2013), Torres and Reeves (2011), numerous others, and my own lived experiences. Researchers suggested that there is not a single leadership theory academics agree on, and that current leadership theories may be outdated, and traditional leadership styles are not maintaining pace with the demands and needs of modern organizational environments (Allio, 2013; Bennett, 2009; Bennis, 2013, Latham, 2014). The data obtained from this study supported Bennis (2013) and Latham's (2014) belief that there was a need to identify and study emerging theory relating to non-traditional leadership practices and identify theories that are no longer relevant or meet the originally envisioned goals.

The Creswell (2014) structured and semi-structured participant interview format was determined to be the most suitable method for gathering research data and was utilized for this study. Prior to use, an interview guide was reviewed by a panel for non-bias open-ended questions that ensured the interviews were designed to address the research questions, purpose of the study, and extract responses from participants that addressed the goals of the study. Participant interviews were recorded, transcribed, and MAXQDA software was utilized for data collection and analysis.

Marshall et al. (2013) suggested that there is not a set or agreed upon sample size for qualitative research; however, they do cite Creswell (2014) who suggested 10-20 participants for a qualitative study. Interviews were conducted over a five-week period during July 2017 through August 2017. O'Reilly and Parker (2013) suggested that during the conduct of research saturation can be satisfied with ten like findings. Initially 20 interviews were planned, however after the first ten interviews, it appeared that saturation had been met. An additional three pre-scheduled interviews were conducted for a total of 13 interviews, which added to the data and confirmation that saturation was satisfied.

Participants for this study were individuals having 20 or more years of experience in the work force with executive level C-suite experience and geographically from all areas of the United States. All participants signed informed consent forms and agreed to audio recording of interviews. Demographic data as shown in table 1 was collected from the participants during the interviews. Four participants were female and nine were males. One participant had a

Bachelor's degree, nine had Masters degrees, and three had Doctorate degrees.

Participants were experienced CEOs, Vice Presidents, Directors, or equivalent positions, and former military participants held Major through General Officer ranks, and enlisted participants were at the E-9 ranks. The age of participants ranged from 45 to 65 years old, and average leadership role experience was 31 years. Participants industry experience was spread across a broad spectrum related to business, marketing, retail, food service, defense, consulting, education, law enforcement, and human resources. For this study anonymity of participants has been maintained and pseudonyms were assigned as P-1 through P-13.

Table 1

Participant Profiles

Pseudonym	Gender	Age	Years Experience	Industry	Current Position	Highest Position	Education
P-1	M	65	41	Business	CEO	Chairman/CEO	Master
P-2	M	61	42	Defense & Consulting	Owner	General US Army	Master
P-3	F	42	21	Mgt Consulting	Sr VP	Sr VP	Master
P-4	M	41	17	Education	Professor	Professor	Doctorate
P-5	M	57	25	Defense	Student	E-9 USAF	Master
P-6	M	63	41	Civel Eng / Defense	President	LTC USAF	Doctorate
P-7	M	65	42	Defense	Retired	Major US Army	Master
P-8	F	45	22	Human Rsources	VP	Vice President	Master
P-9	M	64	43	Defense / Consulting	Owner	General US Army	Master
P-10	M	46	22	Mgt Consulting	Sr VP	President	Master
P-11	M	60	38	Defense / Law Enforcement	Sheriff	Colonel Army	Master
P-12	F	51	25	Food Service	Owner	Vice President	B.S.
P-13	F	55	30	Mgt Consulting / Education	Director	CEO	Doctorate

Results

The below sections present a summary of the research findings. Continual change, conflicting and outdated theories, and trait approach to leadership were the three themes of the research. There were three research questions.

Research Question 1. What events or phenomenon, if any, are causing leaders to practice non-traditional leadership?

The research question sub-questions were: (1) leadership theory practiced, (2) variations of leadership theories practiced, (3) events or circumstances that caused a change in practice, (4) have leaders transitioned from traditional to non-traditional leadership due a specific phenomenon or other event. The responses to these four questions aligned RQ1. Responses to each sub-question provided data that answered RQ1 and showed that the participants were non-traditional leaders and that their motives for their leadership practices were based on a variety of phenomena.

Theories, Phenomenon, and Transition. The first question asked of Participants was intended to determine what knowledge, if any, participants had about leadership theory regardless of their level of leadership knowledge, what were they practicing, and if that practice equated to a traditional leadership theory or style, or non-traditional. At the start of the interview, the terms traditional and non-traditional were explained to participants.

During the first interview with P-1 it was surprising and interesting that his response to the question "What leadership theory/style do you practice" was:

"I think academics like to put these things into buckets. You know you're one of them, you're one of those… it's not the way I think. I don't know how many leaders do."

P1 has 37 years in chairman and CEO level roles for companies recognized by Fortune 500 and Standard & Poor's 500. His experience has ranged from marketing, fast food, and retail companies. P1 expressed a career of practicing non-traditional leadership, and much of his explanations by definition would be considered traits associated across multiple leadership theories such as transformational, transactional, adaptive, full range, and situational.

All the other participants, except for P-4, responded as non-traditional practitioners. P-4 is an Assistant Professor of human resource and organizational leadership at a top ten ranked University with 17 years tenure and considered himself a transformational leader. Given his experience, academic position, and answers to this and other questions, I found his responses interesting. While P-4s considered himself as a transformational leader, his discussion for this question and other questions during the interview suggested that he was a practitioner of multiple styles such as full range, transactional, adaptive, and situational. There was clearly a difference of opinion or definition as to what a transformational leader is, and P4s responses would suggest that he is a non-traditional leader.

The range of leadership experience for participants was 21 to 42 years and averaged 31 years. An assumption could be made that given a span of forty years, leaders would have practiced some form of traditional leadership theory, however the majority of these participants stated they always, or mostly always practiced non-traditional leadership. Table 2 illustrates that a similarity with all participants was during the first years of their respective careers they were exposed to authoritarian and transactional leadership practices, and due to their starting positions and inexperience briefly practiced authoritarian or transactional leadership. All six of the participants who had military service stated being introduced to both authoritarian and transactional leadership, however as their careers progressed, they transitioned to non-traditional practices. All participants stated that during most of their careers through the present they have been non-traditional leaders, and in some instances, were a combination of transformational and non-traditional. A point of interest was that participants did not state being exposed to or practiced transformational leadership during their early career years. The views of the participants were echoed by a quote by P1:

"There is no one formula or cookie cutter approach to effective leadership."

Table 2

RQ1 Leadership Theories Practiced

	P1	P2	P3	P4	P5	P6	P7	P8	P9	P10	P11	P12	P13
Early Career													
Authoritarian /Autocratic	X	X			X	X	X		X		X		
Transactional	X	X	X	X	X	X	X	X	X	X	X	X	X
Transformational													
Majority of Career - Present													
Traditional	X	X			X	X	X	X					
Non-traditional	X	X	X			X	X	X	X	X	X	X	X

In hindsight participants noted inexperience and youth as a reason for using authoritarian or transactional leadership methods. Regarding authoritarian leadership P5 stated:

"I blame this on inexperience. When I was young in the service and I was first given personnel to supervise and lead, it was more of an authoritarian style, it was more directed and then ultimately it just didn't work out. You have to get people engaged and have to communicate with people and you have to include them."

A common view expressed by participants was their dislike for transactional leadership and their view that it was non-inclusive means of leadership. P3 stated that: "I only did transactional when I was a project manager for a project where there were people that were reporting directly to me and it was horrible, it failed miserably. That's one of the problems with that one."

An unexpected finding during data analysis was that many of the answers from research question 1 overlapped into research questions 2. The advancements of technology, social media, stakeholder involvement and interest in how organizations are operated, and work life balance, was a common theme with all participants as to the phenomenon requiring a shift from traditional to non-traditional leadership. One participant stated:

"The people graduating from business schools today have a completely different mindset than the people who graduate from business schools back in the 70s in terms of how they want to be treated and the things they want to do, what their expectations are, and how they think about work life balance."

When participants were asked if they think that today's leaders have transitioned from traditional leadership, their responses were similar in that they themselves and some others are non-traditional, however there are other leaders who have not or will not change. An interesting point was that participants perceived continued practice of traditional leadership as a negative, as stated by P1, P3, and P10:

"The world has changed a lot and leaders have to change with that world. The answer is some organizations are better than others, some people are better than others at adjusting to the change, but the change is happening whether you like it or not. So, if you're going to be successful you better adjust, you have to."

"I think that the majority of leaders are still traditional leadership and they're not going to go to nontraditional leadership practices because it's not easy to grasp and it doesn't feel comfortable."

"I think the successful ones have and I think there are still some industries where that has not occurred and may never occur."

Research Question 2. How are stakeholders' expectations, if any, influencing leadership transition towards non-traditional leadership practices?

The research question sub-questions were: (1) if they believe there are barriers that prevent or make it difficult to be effective leaders, (2) are there organizational, societal, or stakeholder factors that impede their ability to be an effective leader, (3) are there any weaknesses that they cannot control due to the organizational environment or stakeholder expectations, and, (4) do stakeholder expectations have any influence on how they lead. The responses to these four questions aligned with RQ2. The sub-questions design was intended to and did provide data that suggested that elements such as stakeholders views towards change, transparency, generational, technology, social media, and public versus private companies had an impact on how leaders perform today in contrast to how leaders performed in prior decades. Table 3 illustrates the attributes and elements mentioned by participants during their interviews.

Table 3

RQ2 Stakeholder Expectations and/or Influence

	P1	P2	P3	P4	P5	P6	P7	P8	P9	P10	P11	P12	P13
Adaptibility	X	X	X	X	X	X		X	X	X			X
Budget	X	X				X	X		X	X	X		
Change	X	X	X	X	X			X	X	X	X	X	X
Engagement	X	X		X	X	X		X	X	X	X		X
Fear	X	X		X	X	X		X	X	X			X
Generational	X	X	X	X	X	X	X	X	X	X	X		X
Restrictive Innovation	X	X				X			X	X			X
Social Media	X	X	X			X		X	X	X	X	X	X
Technology	X	X	X	X	X	X	X	X	X	X	X	X	X
Transparency	X	X			X	X	X			X	X		
Wall Street/Private vs Public	X	X				X			X	X			X

Barriers. A leader's inability to change was noted as a barrier. A common theme with participants was their acknowledgement that adaptability, or ability and willingness to change was identified as a necessary attribute for a leader to be successful in a constantly changing environment. P1 stated "…change is happening whether you like it or not. So, if you're going to be successful you better adjust, you have to." An interesting point was made by the two General Officer participants in their belief that change was not just something that happens, but that it is a duty of leaders to drive change. P2 stated: "Every critical leader needs to understand that leader's traits and abilities are to make transformational change within the unit to keep the unit running the way it's supposed to be running."

Budget. A surprising response by half of the participants was their input relating to budgets being a barrier. Today's leaders are expected to meet financial goals inclusive with budgets constraints while maintaining transparency and producing profits. Several participants had experience in both public and private organizations, and as noted by P1: "About half of the time that I have been a CEO, I've been the CEO of a public company, and about half the time a private company, and I can tell you there are remarkable differences when it comes to expectations." There was a distinction made between the expectation of profit versus progress, and expressed by P1 and P10 that there is a restriction of innovation placed on public companies due to profit expectation. P10 stated: "if I think about public companies, the stakeholders are Wall Street and shareholders and I think there's an obscene amount of focus on every three months showing progress" and "I think the majority of companies are kind of holding back from innovating and truly being visionary because, if they're not showing that quarterly progress the way Wall Street wants, they're paralyzed and that's a real shame."

Culture, Change and Fear. The majority of participants interchanged culture, change, and fear in their responses as a barrier and impeding a leader's ability to lead. P10 stated: "But I also think in older organizations, where you have sort of that that boys club or you know a culture of we don't change, it's always been this way, and that can be a real barrier because people can perceive it as impossible to overcome." This impression was echoed by several participants who expressed that fear, or some form of fear, restricted leaders from being more innovative, and placed limitations on their ability to perform. Fear was not necessarily the key word, but rather a combination of resistance to change due to fear of change, the internal culture which restricted change, or fear of transparency and the implications of scrutiny if something was interpreted incorrectly.

Generational, Social Media, Technology, Transparency and Engagement. All participants expressed that generational, social media, technology, transparency, and engagement, were all contributing factors to a leader's ability, or inability to effectively lead. These five elements are linked and acceptance and adapting to them was considered necessary. Generational change was considered an important concept that leaders must understand and accept, and with that an understanding that leaders must embrace how social media, technology, transparency, and engagement is part of the generational shift and needs to be incorporated into leadership. P4 stated: "As the leader of a classroom I notice that people expect less lecture today more engagement," and P5 stated: "You have to get people engaged and have to communicate with people, and you have to include them."

Technological advancements were considered as positives for enhancing organizational operations, however, it was also noted that technology has negative aspects to it when leaders communicate. P13 stated: "I think team leaders today depend upon their technology to accomplish things instead of doing the face-to-face leadership things that they need to do" and "Technology use of email and text messaging has created unrealistic expectation for responses." P13's points were echoed by the other participants who noted that while technology has good points, the advancements of social media has created an environment where stakeholders expect instance responses and immediate transparency, and in doing so have eliminated the human element, making it an unrealistic expectation.

Research Question 3.   What concepts or other elements of traditional leadership theory, if any, are practiced within non-transitional leadership practices?

The research question sub-questions were: (1) What concepts, traits or other elements of the traditional leadership theories, if any, do you practice? (2) Are there any leadership training, theories, or other leadership development programs you think are outdated or do not provide the value originally intended? (3) Can you describe in one sentence what makes you an effective leader? (4) What are your views regarding the future of how leadership research, development, and practices should be approached?   The responses to these four questions aligned with RQ3. The sub-questions design provided data that answered RQ3 and suggested that leaders are utilizing multiple elements of various leadership theories. Table 4 illustrates a list of terms identified by five or more participants that feel are important characteristics or traits for leaders to possess and/or practice.

Table 4

RQ3 Leadership Elements, Traits, Outdated Theory, Future of Leadership

	P1	P2	P3	P4	P5	P6	P7	P8	P9	P10	P11	P12	P13
Adaptibility	X	X	X	X	X	X	X	X	X	X			X
Change	X	X	X		X	X	X	X	X	X	X	X	X
Character	X	X		X	X	X	X	X	X	X	X		X
Communication	X	X			X			X	X		X	X	X
Dedication		X				X			X		X		X
Digital Natives / Tech	X	X	X	X		X		X	X	X			X
Emotional Intellgience	X	X		X		X		X	X	X			X
Engagement	X	X		X	X	X		X	X			X	X
Honesty	X	X		X	X	X	X	X	X	X	X	X	X
Integrity	X	X		X	X	X	X	X	X	X	X	X	X
Intelligent	X		X		X	X		X	X	X	X		X
Lisatening	X	X		X	X	X	X	X	X	X	X	X	X
Not the Sartest in the room	X	X		X	X	X		X	X	X			X
Passion	X					X	X	X		X	X	X	X
Resiliency		X			X	X	X	X	X		X		X
Selfless		X			X	X			X				X
Trust	X	X	X	X	X	X			X	X	X		X

Leadership Practices and Effectiveness. A review of the interviews provided data that suggested that all the participants are practitioners of varying leadership theories and do not rely on, or practice, one standalone leadership theory. As table 4 shows, there are numerous elements, traits, and concepts that the participants possess, utilize, or feel are important aspects for leadership. As discussed for RQ2, adaptability and change were identified by most participants as an important skill for effective leaders. Listening and communication were mentioned frequently during interviews and viewed as one of more important skills for a leader. Participant expressed similar views to what P5's stated: "I think the most important thing that a leader should be able to do is communicate leadership with verbal communication skills, and not only should the leader have good verbal communication skills, but a leader should also be able to write well. Accuracy, brevity, and clarity, go a long way with getting the right message."

Participants identified numerous personal characteristics and traits they believed to be important attributes for leaders. Participants mentioned character, dedication, emotional intelligence, honesty, integrity, passion, resiliency, selflessness, trust, and several others as some of the characteristics or traits they felt were important for leaders. The listings were spread across a broad spectrum of attributes identified as elements of multiple leadership theories, such as transformational, transactional, situational, full-range, servant, and participative leadership.

Many participants had a personal philosophy and belief that it is important to surround themselves with smart and intelligent people. P13 stated "I am a very strong believer in surrounding yourself with high performers, people that are very smart people that are very ambitious," and P10 stated "I am a very strong believer in surrounding yourself with high performers, people that are very smart people that are very ambitious. people that are experts and then making sure that they know that you know your success and their success is a symbiotic relationship."

The term digital native was mentioned by P9, whose definition was about the millennial generation and how digital technology and change is normal for them. P9 stated: "I think you must understand generational differences within the formation of your organization. You know most everybody talks about millennials and the differences, and there are differences. I mean we've all grown up differently, you know my kids are millennials. They are what I call digital natives. I'm a digital refugee." The other participants did not use the term digital native, however they shared the same views regarding generational change and belief that members of the millennial generation are technology driven, and to engage them, leaders must adapt and accept that we live in a digital world.

Outdated Theories and Value. The question presented was "Is there any leadership training, theories, or other leadership development programs you think are outdated or do not provide the value originally intended? The participants produced a variety of responses. The responses by participants were diverse, however echoed a similar theme and opinion that leadership theories, training, and development were outdated and required improvement.

One common viewpoint was that it may not be as much as the theories being outdated, but a resistance by people to accept change and implement theory with advances in technology and operating requirements. In some instances, leaders tend to resist change and want to remain in the confines of existing theory while expecting positive results. P2s example was: "I think that what's outdated is the people who to look at the efficiency of an operation outside the concept that the effect of this operation… And so, there's examples of things that are usually outdated by pushing the envelope so far that you throw out the baby with the bathwater."

Research questions one and two provided data that suggested that the participants were not practitioners of the traditional leadership theories and practiced their own methods utilizing elements of multiple leadership theories. Research question three provided similar results relating to outdated theories and lack of value. An interesting point stated by P6 was the separation of senior leadership and middle to lower management. P6 stated: "I don't think the folks sitting in the C-Suite really pay attention to those because their motivation is different and so the leadership theories apply to middle managers, not so much senior managers who were the core of the C-suite to corporate level guys. So, in that regard, they don't really provide value." A common theme with most participants was that senior level leaders do not pay attention to theory.

P13, a university director of a master's in leadership program, shared her view that theories in general are outdated and fragmented:

"I think any of them as a way, like transactional leadership for example as a single solitary approach, that's outdated. We have other nontraditional formats because we pull on the micro properties that are used, and embed them into a systems approach, and we factor in other dimensions of leadership, focusing on taking in appreciative inquiry approach where actually the leader is a factor as part of the team. So, I think essentially, I would approach this question by saying that leadership is being confused with management, is out of date, and leadership focused on you being a leader and as you having a leadership job, as opposed to a leadership role focusing on a manager and the difference between management and leadership and what a leader does. The fact that what their role is, is convoluted."

P13s comments demonstrate that some members of academia acknowledge that traditional leadership theories are outdated and are putting forth their own efforts to address the issue. The outdated theory question was expanded into graduate education by P10 who stated:

"I think the traditional MBA curriculum probably could use an update to the modern world and some schools probably do a better job of that than others. But I think there's still a lot of old school theory that is just pounded into people's head."

A common response to the training and development part of the question, apart from the military, suggested that participants believed there was a lack of, and no valuable leadership training or development established as a requirement for leaders. P11, a thirty-year Army Officer who transitioned into state government and later county sheriff, made the observation about state level government agencies:

"We really don't have good leadership development programs."

What makes you an effective leader? Participants identified numerous and multiple attributes that they believed made them effective leaders. All participants had similar perceptions as to what attributes effective leaders should possess. Adaptability, communication, dedication, experience, and several other attributes as illustrated in table 5 were the most mentioned by participants either for this question, or previous sections of the interviews. In some instances, specific characteristics may not have been mentioned, however similar words expressing the same sentiment were stated, such as for dedication, words like commitment, loyalty, and devotion were stated as effective leadership characteristics. A similarity to the golden rule was given by P1 when he stated:

"The best advice I ever got was from my Dad. The advice he gave me I still think of just about every day. He said, "Well Dave, I think the secret to being a good leader is you have to find out how people want to be treated and treat them that way." That's kind of a guideline that I follow, different people want to be treated different ways. They all have their own personalities, got their own things they respond to. One person responds to a certain kind of leadership direction and other people it's no different for them in that, and I think my dad was very wise in that regard because I really try to think about if I were on the other side of this table, and I were you, how would I want to be treated in this set of circumstances. That's what I try to respond to and that's worked reasonably well for me."

P1 also stated that: *"Effective leaders need to adapt to their circumstance"* and *"There is no one formula or cookie cutter approach to effective leadership."*

P11 stated: *"I think what makes me an effective leader today is that I tore my heart into the job and fiercely dedicated to something I signed up to do."*

P3 stated: *"I am relatable and transparent."*

Table 5

Effective Leader Attributes

Eddective Leader	P1	P2	P3	P4	P5	P6	P7	P8	P9	P10	P11	P12	P13
Adaptibility	X	X	X	X	X	X	X	X	X	X			X
Character	X	X		X	X	X	X	X	X	X	X		X
Communication	X	X			X			X	X		X	X	X
Dedication	X	X	X		X	X	X		X		X		X
Emotional Intellgience	X	X		X		X		X	X	X			X
Engagement	X	X		X	X	X		X	X	X		X	X
Experience	X	X	X		X		X	X	X	X	X		X
Honesty	X	X		X	X	X	X	X	X	X	X	X	X
Integrity	X	X		X	X	X	X	X	X	X	X	X	X
Lisatening	X	X		X	X	X	X	X	X	X	X	X	X

Future of Leadership. The question "What are your views regarding the future of how leadership research, development, and practices should be approached?" was presented to participants. There was a consensus that there was a need for change. Some participants had specific ideas for approaching the future of leadership while others did not know. A common theme of generational emerged from this question. During this question and throughout each section of the interviews, generational changes were mentioned.

Another common theme that emerged was related to adaptability, change, and the advancements in technology and organizational environments. P12 answered *"More culturally sensitive, more globalization"* as a need for the future leadership to develop. Another participant commented that he believed that current leadership theory is unrelatable to current and upcoming leadership responsibilities. Although budget barriers were discussed previously, the topic along with resistance to change were identified as subjects that needed addressing for future leadership development. Budget driven priorities in public companies versus innovation and progress were discussed as barriers that needed to be overcome. The budget issue was connected to resistance to change, and participants believed that overcoming resistance to change was a contributor to leader's inability to maximize both their personal potential as leaders, and the potential of companies they worked for.

Generally, participants shared a common view that the future of leadership was dependent upon acceptance of generational shifts, and adjusting of leadership theories, budget barrier and resistance to change. Table 6 illustrates elements that the majority of participants identified as requirement for future leadership requirements.

Table 6

Future of Leadership Constraints

Future of Leadership	P1	P2	P3	P4	P5	P6	P7	P8	P9	P10	P11	P12	P13
Generational	X	X	X	X	X	X	X	X	X	X	X	X	X
Outdated	X	X			X	X	X	X	X	X	X	X	X
Budget barriers	X	X			X	X	X	X	X	X	X		
Resistance to change	X	X	X	X	X	X	X	X	X	X	X	X	X

Evaluation of Findings

A phenomenological qualitative research approach was conducted for this study utilizing the unstructured and semi-structured interview format. The purpose of this qualitative study was to ascertain if organizational leaders have transitioned from academically recommended leadership theories to their own non-traditional leadership practices. Participants were provided instructions detailing that for this study the term traditional leadership was defined as traditional leadership theories such as authoritarian, transactional, transformational, and other established theories that are practiced independently from one another. The term non-traditional leadership was defined as individual practices or developed methods, other approaches, or combining different elements from the various traditional leadership theories into their own practices. Data collected from thirteen participants during the interviews identified emerging themes relating to their respective experiences and views regarding leadership.

Themes. The primary themes for this study were: (1) continually changing organizational environment, (2) conflicting leadership theories, and (3) trait approach to leadership. Three research questions were developed for this study, with each research question consisting of four sub-questions for a total of twelve questions. Participants were also offered the opportunity to add any additional information they believed would contribute to the study.

The research revealed a surprising finding related to the three themes. As shown in table 7, all participants had expressed an understanding and in some form a working knowledge of the three themes. All participants viewed continual change as an ongoing phenomenon that has required leaders to continually adapt while accepting change. Participants expressed their beliefs that many or all leadership theories were outdated. Participants stated their views relating to traits and belief that a broad range of attributes are necessary for leaders to be successful. These participants appeared to have embraced an apparent common viewpoint and practice, as Kouzes and Posner (2012) suggested, that leaders have evolved and practice multiple leadership theories simultaneously, evident by the practice of common traits found across numerous leadership styles.

Table 7

Themes

Themes	P1	P2	P3	P4	P5	P6	P7	P8	P9	P10	P11	P12	P13
Continually Changing Environment	X	X	X	X	X	X	X	X	X	X	X	X	X
Conflicting Leadership Theories	X	X	X	X	X	X	X	X	X	X	X	X	X
Trait Approach to Leadership	X	X	X	X	X	X	X	X	X	X	X	X	X

The phenomenon of continually changing organizational environments has emerged in recent years and expected to continue into the future (Dew et al., 2011; Torres & Reeves, 2013). Bennis (2014) suggested that leadership had been fundamentally changed due to globalization, technology, and digitization. This sentiment was echoed by the interview participants, all of whom expressed that their own personal leadership practices and their observations of other leaders had evolved within an environment of continual change. Although a direct question was not asked, interview participants revealed a personal belief that there existed a phenomenon of an evolving and constant progress within society affecting all aspects of global interaction, economics, business, and organizational environments (Dew et al., 2011; Torres & Reeves, 2013).

An interesting finding from the interviews was an awareness and acceptance of a term called generational. Participants were aware of changes in society and expressed a similar view to Anderson's (2016) that the continual growth of the younger generations presents unusual situations, attitudes, and personality differences that impact leadership approaches. Participants further expressed an understanding that for leaders to be successful, they must accept change, and adapt to continuous changes in technology and hold a strong advantage over both their older counterparts, and their leaders who have difficulties adapting (Kaifi, et al., 2012).

There are conflicting views concerning transformational, transactional, and other leadership theories, their applications, and the overall study of leadership (Latham, 2014). McCleskey (2014) and Silva (2014) suggested that there in not a single effective leadership style, and there are conflicting perceptions and viewpoints regarding leadership by academia, academic researchers and organizations where traditional leadership is practiced. During the interview, twelve of the thirteen participants identified themselves as non-traditional practitioners, and shared similar views relating to the ineffectiveness of applying traditional leadership theory to organizational leadership. The participant who considered himself a traditional leader, shared very similar experiences, practices and views of leadership as the other participants, and even though he considered himself a traditional leader, an analysis of his interview would imply he was a non-traditional leader.

Each participant shared a personal belief that for a leader to be successful, a variety of attributes were required. As previously shown in table 4, participants stated their belief that leaders should possess and/or be capable of adaptability, change, communication, listening, honesty, integrity, and numerous other attributes. All participants either mentioned emotional intelligence, or various definitions of emotional intelligence regarding a requirement for leaders.

Research Question 1. The data produced from RQ1 was surprising and exceeded anticipated expectations for this study. The premise for this study was a view that a large portion of today's leaders were practitioners of non-traditional leadership instead of the suggested and recommended traditional leadership theories. Participants were recruited from a wide range of industries to solicit data from a broad base of professionals not restricted to one specialty.

Illustrated in table 8, the data solicited from the participants, either by direct statements, or by their own explanations of how they lead, revealed that all the thirteen participants are currently practitioners of non-traditional leadership and do not limit themselves to a single or specific traditional leadership theory. A majority of participants shared their observations and opinions concerning other leaders and expressed similar beliefs that for leaders to be successful, they had to practice non-traditional leadership methods. An interesting point concerning this data is if we assume the participants represent a cross section of today's leaders, and because all the participants are practitioners of non-traditional leadership, it can be argued that all leaders practice non-traditional leadership. This finding would create a question for further research as to the continued recommended practices of traditional leadership theories.

Table 8

Theory Practiced Today

Theory Practiced Today	P1	P2	P3	P4	P5	P6	P7	P8	P9	P10	P11	P12	P13
Stated Practice: Traditional				X									
Stated Practice: Non-traditional	X	X	X		X	X	X	X	X	X	X	X	X
Actual Practice: Non-traditional	X	X	X	X	X	X	X	X	X	X	X	X	X

Research Question 2. This question provided anticipated data, however it also produced two unexpected findings. Direct questions about budgets and generational or millennials were not asked, however, participants introduced these two categories. Budget limitations were identified as a hindrance to both leadership performance and organizational efficiency. A distinction was made between public and private companies and a consensus that public companies were short term profit driven versus innovation driven, whereas private companies were long term innovation driven.

All participants introduced and expressed an understanding of generational differences and change. Anderson (2016) suggested that a challenge for organizational leadership is generational differences between the older generation, and the younger generations, a sentiment that all participants were aware of and embraced. The term digital native was introduced by one participant, referring to how millennials have grown up with technology, and adapt to continuous changes in technology (Hartman & McCambridge, 2011; Piper, 2012). The requirement to understand and adapt to change relating to generational differences was a common theme discussed by all participants.

A combination of emotional intelligence elements and surrounding oneself with smart people was another common theme. Most of the participants noted the importance of surrounding themselves with smart people and believed that it was important to realize that they may not be "the smartest person in the room." This theme was incorporated with elements of emotional intelligence and a practice and belief by participants concerning the importance of communicating, listening, and experience. The absence of these types of emotional intelligence attributes have been identified by researchers as skills that contribute to leadership failure (Kaigh et al., 2014).

Research Question 3. This research question was intended to identify views and practices concerning current applications of leadership theories and traits of participants. Responses produced a broad variety of traits as previously shown in table 4. A common and unexpected finding was that all participants shared similar opinions about the necessity for leaders to be adaptable and capable of accepting change.

The topic of generational was reintroduced during discussion, and participants noted that continual change within generations, technological advances and globalization, required leaders to possess skill sets capable of adapting to these changes. This mindset supports a trend in society where millennials are not the ones that need to adapt because of the social and technological exposure of millennials, adaptability to change is a second nature attribute (Stewart et al., 2016).

Another unexpected finding was that all participants believed that traditional leaderships theories are either not relevant, outdated, or needed improvement. A common theme was the view that there is resistance to change by some leaders, and therefore a desire to stay within the confines of traditional theory. Participants expressed that leadership development or training was non-existent or did not relate to current global organizational environments. Participants shared a common view that the future of leadership was dependent upon acceptance of generational shifts, and adjusting of leadership theories, budget barriers and eliminating resistance to change.

Summary

The purpose of this qualitative study was to ascertain if organizational leaders have transitioned from academically recommended leadership theories to their own non-traditional leadership practices. The data collected and analyzed from this study supports the assertions by Apenko and Chernobaeva (2016), Allio (2013), Bennis (2014), Kouzes and Posner (2012, Latham (2014), Torres and Reeves, (2014), and other researchers, that traditional leadership theories have not maintained pace with changing organizational and global environments. The data also supports the premise that today's leaders are practicing their own self-direct leadership style.

For the purpose of this research the term traditional leadership was defined as traditional leadership theories such as authoritarian, transactional, transformational, and other established theories that are practiced independently from one another. The term non-traditional leadership was defined as individual practices or developed methods, other approaches, or combining different elements from the various traditional leadership theories into their own practices. There were three themes identified for the study: (1) continually changing organizational environment, (2) conflicting leadership theories, and (3) trait approach to leadership.

The research data collected exceeded expectations. The research showed that all the participants had an understanding and working knowledge of the three themes. All participants viewed continual change as an ongoing phenomenon and that many or all leadership theories were outdated. Participants believed that a broad range of attributes are necessary for leaders to be successful and embraced a common perspective that leaders have evolved and practice multiple leadership theories simultaneously (Kouzes & Posner, 2012). An unexpected finding based on the responses and discussions during the interviews was that all thirteen participants currently practice non-traditional leadership.

The inclusion of the term generational, referring to millennials, was another unexpected finding. All participants were aware and understood that due to the social and technological exposure of millennials, adaptability to change was second nature attribute (Stewart et al., 2016). This data supported another finding related to adaptability and change. Participants acknowledged the necessity for leaders to recognize generational differences, and be capable of adaptive leadership, and accept change as the norm versus the exception.

Budgets were another unexpected topic of discussion. A distinction was made between public and private companies and a consensus that public companies were short term profit driven versus innovation driven, and private companies were long term innovation driven. A common theme was that public companies were more restrictive with research and innovation funding and made profits a priority.

Adaptability, change, communication, listening, honesty, integrity, and numerous other attributes were identified by participants as necessary qualities for successful leaders. Emotional intelligence or variations of emotional intelligence was discussed by participants and was considered an important asset for leadership. The emotional intelligence aspect was tied into a common theme of being surrounded by smart people.

Participants shared a common belief that traditional leaderships theories are either not relevant, outdated, or need improvement. This sentiment was the same for leadership development and training, and participants believed it was either non-existent or did not relate to current global organizational environments. Participants shared a common perspective that the future of leadership was dependent upon acceptance of generational shifts, and adjusting of leadership theories, budget barriers and eliminating resistance to change.

Chapter 5

Implications, Recommendations, And Conclusions

The phenomenon of the continually changing organizational environments of the 21st century has resulted in a problem with the continued teaching, recommended use, and continued employment of outdated leadership theories (Bennis, 2013; Latham, 2014). It has been suggested that leaders no longer practice traditional leadership styles and have transitioned towards enhanced leadership approaches including practicing several leadership styles simultaneously, and individually adapted methods (Derue & Wellman, 2009; Kaigh, Driscoll, Tucker, & Lam, 2014; Srinivasan, 2010). The general problem involves a global environment of continuous change associated with technology, globalization, and transparency, which has bypassed traditional leadership theories that were not designed to address the 21st century organizational issues (Bennis, 2013; Latham, 2014; Rietsema & Watkins, 2012). The specific problem was there is a lack of understanding of why organizational leaders have transitioned from academically recommended leadership theories to their own non-traditional leadership practices, a practice not yet associated with a leadership theory or model (Derue & Wellman, 2009; Fibuch, 2011; Kaigh, et al., 2014).

The purpose of this phenomenological qualitative study was to explore why organizational leaders have transitioned from traditional leadership theories to their own non-traditional leadership practices (Derue & Wellman, 2009; Fibuch, 2011; Kaigh, et al., 2014). Interviews with thirteen participants were conducted utilizing the Creswell (2014) structured and semi-structured participant interview format. The interviews produced data based upon the lived experiences of participants that supported emerging theories relating to why leaders have ignored existing recommended leadership theories.

There is extensive research on traditional leadership theories, however there is limited research on the phenomenon of leaders ignoring traditional leadership theory and adopting their own leadership methods (Bennis, 2013; Latham, 2014). The absence of literature on the subject limited the literature review. Additional limitations included the sample size of thirteen participants. Ethical dimensions were considered. Northcentral University Institutional Review Board (IRB) approval was obtained prior to any data collection. Participants' anonymity and all personal information was kept confidential.

This chapter will review the results of the study. Implications will be reviewed first, followed by recommendations. Recommendations will include suggestions for future research on non-traditional leadership practices.

Implications

Three themes were identified for this study: (1) Continual change, (2) conflicting and outdated theories, and (3) trait approach to leadership. The three research questions for this study were: (RQ1) What events or phenomenon, if any, are causing leaders to practice non-traditional leadership? (RQ2) How are stakeholders' expectations, if any, influencing leadership transition towards non-traditional leadership practices? (RQ3) What concepts or other elements of traditional leadership theory, if any, are practiced within non-transitional leadership practices? Review of the participants lived experiences and the literature review provided data to support the themes and research questions of this study.

RQ1. What events or phenomenon, if any, are causing leaders to practice non-traditional leadership?

The premise for this study was in part the problem associated with, and concept that there was an emerging phenomenon that caused some organizational leaders to practice non-traditional leadership instead of traditional leadership theories. This study comprised of thirteen participants. The study results exceeded expectations.

During the interviews it was evident that all participants shared common views as to ongoing phenomenon involving generational changes, technological advancements, globalization, social media, and transparency. An unexpected finding was that participants responses indicated that all participants were practitioners of non-traditional leadership practices (Kouzes & Posner, 2012). A reasonable expectation and assumption were that there would have been that a percentage of participants, as many as fifty percent or more, who would have considered themselves traditional leaders, however it was unexpected to find that all of them considered themselves or provided responses that classified them as non-traditional leaders.

The outcome of the data that revealed participants were non-traditional leaders could imply the possibility that the problem is far more extensive than originally believed. The participants are a cross section from various industries and specialties, and an assumption could be made that their experiences, opinions, and leadership practices may be a common trend for a majority, if not all, organizational leaders.

RQ2. How are stakeholders' expectations, if any, influencing leadership transition towards non-traditional leadership practices?

Data results from RQ1 overlapped in part into RQ2. RQ1 identified a phenomenon that suggested what caused leaders to practice non-traditional leadership. Likewise, these same factors such as continual change in organizational and societal environments, transparency, generational change, technology, and social media, were identified as contributing factors that influenced leader's practices (Bennis, 2014; Torres & Reeves, 2013).

Participants viewed themselves as being adaptive and accepting of a continuously changing world. They noted that resistance to change and the inability of a leader to be adaptable were two barriers to leadership. These two attributes were a necessary requirement for a successful leader. Culture and fear were identified as a reason for leaders' lack of adaptability and resistance to change. Culture and fear were blended together as a reason for resistance to change.

Budgets limitations was another barrier noted by several participants. There was a consensus that public versus private companies had an impact on how leaders perform. In relation to public company's leaders are expected to meet budgetary requirements and financial goals while maintaining transparency and producing profits. Public companies were considered short term profit driven versus innovation driven, and private companies were long term innovation driven. Another point with public companies was that there were more restrictions on research and innovation funding, and profits were the priority.

A leader's inability to understand generational change, transparency, technology, and social media were identified as contributing factors to a leader's inability to effectively lead. These elements are linked and acceptance and adapting to them was considered necessary. A common theme with participants centered on generational change, which was considered an important concept that leaders must understand, and in doing so, will understand that leaders must embrace how transparency, technology, and social media is part of the generational shift and needs to be incorporated into leadership (Anderson et al., 2016; Kaifi, et al., 2012).

RQ3. What concepts or other elements of traditional leadership theory, if any, are practiced within non-transitional leadership practices?

The research data suggested that all participants were practitioners of multiple elements of several leadership theories. The data further suggested that these participants did not depend on or practice one single leadership theory and practiced multiple elements from several established theories. Authoritarian, situational, transactional, and transformational were some of the traditional theories mentioned by participants.

Table 4

RQ3 Leadership Elements, Traits, Outdated Theory, Future of Leadership

	P1	P2	P3	P4	P5	P6	P7	P8	P9	P10	P11	P12	P13
Adaptibility	X	X	X	X	X	X	X	X	X	X			X
Change	X	X	X	X	X	X	X	X	X	X	X	X	X
Character	X	X		X	X	X	X	X	X	X	X		X
Communication	X	X			X			X	X		X	X	X
Dedication		X				X			X		X		X
Digital Natives / Tech	X	X	X	X		X		X	X	X			X
Emotional Intellgience	X	X		X		X		X	X	X			X
Engagement	X	X		X	X	X		X	X	X		X	X
Honesty	X	X		X	X	X	X	X	X	X	X	X	X
Integrity	X	X		X	X	X	X	X	X	X	X	X	X
Intelligent	X		X		X	X		X	X	X	X		X
Lisatening	X	X		X	X	X	X	X	X	X	X	X	X
Not the Sartest in the room	X	X		X	X	X		X	X	X			X
Passion	X					X	X	X		X	X	X	X
Resiliency		X			X	X	X	X	X		X		X
Selfless		X			X	X			X				X
Trust	X	X	X	X	X	X			X	X	X		X

Table 4 provided a list of numerous attributes identified by participants, all of which are associated with various leadership theories. Adaptability and change were the most common attributes mentioned as a requirement for successful leaders. Character, dedication, emotional intelligence, honesty, integrity, passion, resiliency, selflessness, trust, and several other attributes were identified as important for leaders. The listing of attributes was spread across a broad range of attributes identified as elements of multiple leadership theories, such as transformational, transactional, situational, full-range, servant, and participative leadership.

Participants presented similar views relating to outdated leadership theories. Leadership theories, training, and development were considered outdated, not keeping pace with globalization and technological advancements, or required improvement. A common opinion expressed was that resistance to change by leaders was a contributor to outdated theories.

Recommendations for Practice

The research indicated that all participants were practitioners of non-traditional leadership, an unexpected outcome. Proponents of current leadership theory such as transactional and transformational recommended that each leadership style be practiced independently (Allio, 2013; Van Dierendonck & Nuijten, 2011). Avolio (2009) and Ling (2008) suggested that transformational leadership and its associated traits have emerged as the dominant leadership style. Burns (2012), Bennett (2009), Latham (2014), Northouse (2013) and Thompson (2012) suggested that the traits of leadership, including Kouzes and Posner's five practices of exemplary leadership, are not restricted to one single leadership style and can be practiced across multiple leadership styles (Kouzes & Posner, 2017).

The research data suggested that elements from multiple traditional leadership theories were being utilized by participants, and therefore a recommendation would be the continued teaching of traditional theory, however not as independent theories. Elements of traditional theory should be incorporated or blended into a new single style practice, considered non-traditional. It is apparent that leaders have already adopted this concept, and what is needed is a researcher to conduct additional research, analyze the research, and develop the already practiced style into a written and teachable product.

Recommendations for Future Research

Since the data suggested all thirteen participants were not practitioners of traditional leadership theories, the outcome would imply that all, or a majority of leaders across multiple industries are currently practicing non-traditional leadership. Furthermore, it would suggest that all or most leaders no longer practice traditional leadership. These results would be a basis for a wider range of research with a larger number of participants.

The research data could imply that all leaders, not just the participants, practice non-traditional leadership. The participants shared a personal perspective about other leaders, who due to fear and resistance to change, may continue traditional leadership practices. This would indicate the need for further research concerning adaptability and change aspects of leadership. This would also indicate that while the participants in this study are non-traditional leaders, there would likely be traditional leaders who could provide data explaining their rationale relating to their traditional leadership practices. Additionally, the unexpected results that all participants consider themselves non-traditional leaders warrant further research.

Based on the results of this study, it is recommended that further research be conducted. The recommended research is for the purpose of: (1) ascertaining how wide spread the practice of non-traditional leadership practices has evolved, (2) why leaders have chosen to ignore the recommended academic teachings of traditional leadership theories, (4) has professional and academic institutions recognized the phenomenon of leaders shift from traditional leadership, and (5) why do professional and academic institutions ignore emerging leadership practices and phenomenon, and continue to teach and recommend continued traditional leadership practices. Additional research should also be conducted, but limited to traditional leaders, to determine if fear and resistance to change is the reason for continued traditional practices, of if there are other reasons.

Conclusions

The renowned pioneer in the field of leadership, Warren Bennis (2013) believed that leadership has been fundamentally changed due to digitization, globalization, and technology. The suggestions by Bennis has been resonated by other researchers including Latham (2014) and Dew, Enriquez, McFarlane, and Schroeder (2011) who identified the phenomenon of an evolving and constant progression within society affecting all aspects of global interaction, economics, business, and organizational environments. The continued growth of organizational dimensions, globalization, increased stakeholder involvement in organizational affairs, and changes within traditional business practices have created gaps in leadership. New requirements for leaders to possess an adaptive capacity and skill sets to be effective have emerged, and current leadership theories were not designed for, and do not address this issue (Latham, 2014).

This study addressed the issues associated with the phenomenon of continual changing organizational environments, and the problem with continued teaching, recommended use, and continued employment of outdated leadership theories (Bennis, 2013; Latham, 2014). There is extensive research on traditional leadership theories, however there is limited research on the phenomenon of leaders ignoring traditional leadership theory and adopting their own leadership methods (Bennis, 2013; Latham, 2014). There is a specific problem encompassing a lack of research and understanding as to why organizational leaders have transitioned from academically recommended leadership theories to their own non-traditional leadership practices, which has not been addressed with any existing leadership theory or model (Derue & Wellman, 2009; Fibuch, 2011; Kaigh, et al., 2014).

Three themes were identified for the study, (1) Continual change, (2) conflicting and outdated theories, and (3) trait approach to leadership. Three research questions were designed to solicit data that supports Bennis (2013) and Latham's (2014) assertions concerning the need for further research, and the premise that future leaders must adapt and change to be effective leaders. The research questions were also designed to collect data to determine if leaders were practitioners of traditional or non-traditional leadership, and if they were non-traditional, what phenomenon or other events impacted their decisions to practice non-traditional leadership. Traditional leadership was defined as practicing a traditional leadership theory such as authoritarian, transactional, transformational, or other established theories. Non-traditional leadership was defined as practicing a self-developed method or approach, or the blending of various elements from multiple traditional leadership theories.

Creswell (2014) suggested 10-20 participants for a qualitative study, and 13 interview participants were used for this study. Initially 20 interviews were planned, however after the first ten interviews, saturation had been met. An additional three pre-scheduled interviews were conducted for a total of 13 interviews, which added confirmation that saturation was satisfied (O'Reilly & Parker, 2013). As shown in table 1, participants for this study were selected for possessing 20 or more years of experience in multiple work force industries with executive level C-suite experience. Participants were geographically from all areas of the United States.

Table 1

Participant Profiles

Pesudonym	Gender	Age	Years Experience	Industry	Current Position	Highest Position	Education
P-1	M	65	41	Business	CEO	Chairman/CEO	Master
P-2	M	61	42	Defense & Consulting	Owner	General US Army	Master
P-3	F	42	21	Mgt Consulting	Sr VP	Sr VP	Master
P-4	M	41	17	Education	Professor	Professor	Doctorate
P-5	M	57	25	Defense	Student	E-9 USAF	Master
P-6	M	63	41	Civel Eng / Defense	President	LTC USAF	Doctorate
P-7	M	65	42	Defense	Retired	Major US Army	Master
P-8	F	45	22	Human Rsources	VP	Vice President	Master
P-9	M	64	43	Defense / Consulting	Owner	General US Army	Master
P-10	M	46	22	Mgt Consulting	Sr VP	President	Master
P-11	M	60	38	Defense / Law Enforcement	Sheriff	Colonel Army	Master
P-12	F	51	25	Food Service	Owner	Vice President	B.S.
P-13	F	55	30	Mgt Consulting / Education	Director	CEO	Doctorate

This study produced data that, as Bennis (2014) and Latham (2014) suggested, there is a gap between content and teaching of existing leadership theory, and the actual leadership practices of leaders responding to current organizational environments. This study produced both anticipated and unexpected results. There was an expectation that participants from a variety of industries would provide similar responses to some questions related to leadership practices, it was however, unexpected that all participants would indicate being practitioners of non-traditional leadership. Analysis of the data and participants own responses indicated that all participants were non-traditional leaders, were aware of the necessity for adaptability and acceptance to change, and fully aware of generational changes and requirements to be successful. Additionally, participants recognized the phenomenon of continual organizational environmental changes, changing societal environments, social media, transparency, and technology advancements as being critical for leaders to understand (Bennis, 2014; Torres & Reeves, 2013). Culture, fear, and budgets were identified as barriers to successful leadership. A distinction between public and private companies was identified and it was noted that public companies were more profit motivated than innovation motivated, while it was reversed for private companies that were long term focused.

The research data suggested that all study participants utilized multiple elements from several traditional leadership theories, did not rely on one standalone theory, and viewed adaptability and acceptance of change as vital to effective leadership. Character, dedication, emotional intelligence, and numerous other attributes were identified as important for leaders to possess. Participants viewed current leadership theory, training, and development as outdated.

The results of this study would indicate that individual leaders across multiple industries and specializations have recognized a problem with changing environments and have taken it upon themselves to adopt a combination of their own self-developed methods with elements from multiple traditional leadership theories. Based on participant responses, the results suggested that traditional leadership theories are considered outdated and/or do not apply to current organizational environments. The results of the study would also indicate that while traditional leadership theories continue to be taught by professional and academic institutions, the theories themselves are not being practiced and only certain attributes or traits from various theories are implemented or utilized by leaders.

Based on the results of this study, it is recommended that further research be conducted. A broader range of research participants should be conducted to determine if it would produce similar results that suggested all leaders are non-traditional. Additional research should be conducted to evaluate how widespread the practice of non-traditional leadership practices has spread and why leaders have chosen to ignore the recommended academic teachings of traditional leadership theories. Further research should be conducted concentrating on traditional leaders, in an effort to understand their motivations for following traditional leadership models.

References

Aga, D. A. (2016). transactional leadership and project success: The moderating role of goal clarity. *Procedia Computer Science, 100*(International Conference on ENTERprise Information Systems/International Conference on Project Management/International Conference on Health and Social Care Information Systems and Technologies, CENTERIS/ProjMAN / HCist 2016), 517-525. doi:10.1016/j.procs.2016.09.190

Al-Khasawneh, A., & Futa, S. (2013). The impact of leadership styles used by the academic staff in the Jordanian public universities on modifying students' behavior: A field study in the northern region of Jordan. *International Journal of Business and Management, 8*(1), 1-10. doi: http://dx.doi.org/10.5539/ijbm.v8n1p1

Allio, R. J. (2013). Leaders and leadership: Many theories, but what advice is reliable? *Strategy & Leadership, 41*(1), 4-14. doi:10.1108/10878571311290016

Alsaeedi, F., & Male, T. (2013). Transformational leadership and globalization: Attitudes

of school principals in America. *Educational Management Administration &*
Leadership, 41(5), 640-657. doi:10.1177/1741143213488588

Anderson, H. J., Baur, J. E., Griffith, J. A., & Buckley, M. R. (2016). What works for you may not work for (Gen)Me: Limitations of present leadership theories for the new generation. *The Leadership Quarterly*, doi:10.1016/j.leaqua.2016.08.001

Anderson, M. H., & Sun, P. T. (2017). Reviewing leadership styles: Overlaps and the need for a new 'full-range' theory. *International Journal Of Management Reviews*, *19*(1), 76-96. doi:10.1111/ijmr.12082

Andibo, A. E. (2012). Gender disparities in leadership: Societal perceptions, women's capabilities and UASU'S stand. *Journal of Emerging Trends in Educational Research and Policy Studies, 3*(3), 280-286. Retrieved from http://journals.co.za/content/sl_jeteraps/3/3/EJC140945

Andressen, P., Konradt, U., & Neck, C. P. (2012). The relation between self-leadership and transformational leadership: Competing models and the moderating role of virtuality. *Journal of Leadership & Organizational Studies*, *19*(1), 68-82. doi:10.1177/1548051811425047

Anderson, W., Curley, M., & Formica, P. (2010). *Knowledge-driven entrepreneurship, Knowledge Management 102.*

doi:10.1007/978-1-4419-1188-9_9.   New   York,   NY:
Springer.

Anfara, V., & Mertz, N. (2015). *Theoretical frameworks in qualitative research* (2nd ed.). Thousand Oaks, CA: Sage.

Apenko, S., & Chernobaeva, G. (2016). The influence of complex adaptive leadership on the efficiency of business management. *Proceedings Of The European Conference On Management, Leadership & Governance*, 17-24. Retrieved from http://www.academic-conferences.org/

Auger, G. A. (2014). Trust me, trust me not: An experimental analysis of the effect of transparency on organizations. *Journal of Public Relations Research*, *26*(4), 325-343. doi:10.1080/1062726X.2014.908722

Avolio, B. J., Sosik, J. J., Kahai, S. S., & Baker, B. (2014). E-leadership: Re-examining transformations in leadership source and transmission. *The Leadership Quarterly*, *25*(Leadership Quarterly 25th Anniversary Issue), 105-131. doi:10.1016/j.leaqua.2013.11.003

Avolio, B., Walumbwa, F. & Weber, T. (2009). Leadership: Current theories, research, and future directions. *Annual Review of Psychology*, *60*, 421-449. doi: 10.1146/annurev.psych.60.110707.163621

Avolio, B., Lawler, J., Shi, K., Walumbwa, F. & Wang, P. (2005). Transformational leadership and work-related attitudes: The moderating effects of collective and self-efficacy across cultures. *Journal of Leadership & Organizational Studies, 11*(3), 2-16. doi:10.1177/107179190501100301

Avolio, B. J., Bass, B. M., & Jung, D. I. (1999). Re-examining the components of transformational and transactional leadership using the Multifactor Leadership Questionnaire. *Journal of Occupational and Organizational Psychology, 72*, 441-462

Ayman, R., & Korabik, K. (2010). Why gender and culture matter. *American Psychologist, 65*, 157-170. doi: 10.1037/a0018806

Balyer, A. (2012). Transformational leadership behaviors of school principals: A qualitative research based on teachers' perceptions. *International Online Journal of Educational Sciences*, 4(3), 581-591. Retrieved from http://www.iojes.net

Bass, B. M. (1985). *Leadership and performance beyond expectations*. New York, NY: Free Press.

Bass, B. M. (1997). Does the transactional–Transformational paradigm transcend organizational and national boundaries? *American Psychologist, 22*, 130–142. doi:10.1037/0003-066X.52.2.130

Bass, B.M., & Avolio, B.J. (2004). *MLQ-5X multifactor leadership questionnaire* (3rd ed.). Redwood City, CA: Mind Garden.

Bass, B. M., & Bass, R. (2008*). The Bass handbook of leadership: Theory, research, and managerial applications.* SimonandSchuster.com.

Bennett, T. M. (2009). A study of the management leadership style preferred by it subordinates. *Journal of Organizational Culture, Communication and Conflict, 13*(2), 1-25. Retrieved from http://www.alliedacademies.org/index.php

Bennis, W. G. (2009). *On becoming a leader* (4th ed.). New York: Basic Books.

Bennis, W. G. (2013). Leadership in a digital world: Embracing transparency and adaptive capacity. *MIS Quarterly, 37*(2), 635-636. Retrieved from http://www.misq.org/skin/frontend/default/misq/pdf/V37I2/S I_DBS_BharadwajI&O.pdf

Bhatti, N., Murta Maitlo, G., Shaikh, N., Hashmi, M. A., & Shaikh, F. M. (2012). The impact of autocratic and democratic leadership style on job satisfaction. *International Business Research, 5*(2), 192-201. Retrieved from http://www.ccsenet.org/journal/index.php/ibr/article/view/14 599

Blanchard, K. H., & Hersey, P. (1996). Life-cycle theory of leadership. *Training & Development*, *50*42-47.

Boateng, C. (2012). Evolving conceptualization of leadership and its implication for vocational technical education. *World Journal of Education*, *2*(4), 45-54. doi: https://doi.org/10.5430/wje.v2n4p45

Boddy, C. R. (2016). Sample size for qualitative research. *Qualitative Market Research: An International Journal*, *19*(4), 426. doi:10.1108/QMR-06-2016-0053

Brothers, J. T., & Schnurman-Crook, A. (2015). Art in the dark: Using adaptive leadership pedagogy for undergraduate leadership development. *Journal of Leadership, Accountability and Ethics*, *12*(5), 43-47. Retrieved from http://www.na-businesspress.com/JLAE/jlaescholar.html

Burns, J. M. (1978). *Leadership.* New York, NY: Harper & Row.

Bush, S., Erlich, A., Prather, L., Zeira, Y. (2016). The effects of authoritarian iconography: An experimental test. *Comparative Political Studies*. doi: 10.1177/0010414016633228

Carter, T. (2013). Global leadership. *Journal of Management Policy and Practice*, *14*(1), 69-74. Retrieved from www.na-businesspress.com/JMPP/CarterT_Web14_1_.pdf

Calik, T., Sezgin, F., Kavgaci, H., & Cagatay, A. (2012). Examination of relationships between instructional leadership of school principals and self-efficacy of teachers and collective teacher efficacy. *Educational Sciences: Theory and Practice, 12*(4), 2498-2504. Retrieved from http://www.edam.com.tr/estp.asp

Celarent, B. (2014). Review of An outline of a theory of civilization. *American Journal of Sociology, 119*(4), 1213-1220. doi:10.1086/675670

Chase, M., Jacob, J., Jacob, M., Perry, M. & Von Laue, T. (2013). Western Civilization: Ideas, politics, and society. Boston, MA: Cengage Learning.

Chism, B., & Pang, V. (2014). Transforming education and supporting equity through opportunity to learn standards. *National Forum of Applied Educational Research Journal, 27*(1), 19-30. Retrieved from http://www.nationalforum.com

Clark, K. R. (2017). Managing Multiple Generations in the Workplace. *Radiologic Technology, 88*(4), 379-398. Retrieved from https://www.asrt.org/

Clark, M. (2009). What got you here won't get you there: How successful people become even more successful. *Academy of Management Perspectives, 23*(3), 103-105. doi:10.5465/AMP.2009.43479273

Colbert, T., Judge, T., Choi, D. & Wang, G. (2012). Assessing the trait theory of leadership using self and observer ratings of personality: The mediating role of contributions to group success. *Leadership Quarterly, 23* (4), 670–685. doi:10.1016/j.leaqua.2012.03.004

Collinson, D., & Tourish, D. (2015). Teaching leadership critically: New directions for leadership pedagogy. *Academy of Management Learning & Education, 14*(4), 576-594. doi:10.5465/amle.2014.0079

Cowan, L. D. (2014). e-Leadership: Leading in a virtual environment -- Guiding principles for nurse leaders. *Nursing Economic$,* 32(6), 312-322.

Creswell, J. W. (2014). *Research design: Qualitative, quantitative, and mixed methods approaches* (4th ed.). Thousand Oaks, CA: Sage.

Creswell, J. W. (2012). *Qualitative inquiry & research design: Choosing among five approaches* (3rd ed.). Thousand Oaks, CA: Sage.

Cruz, M. P., Nunes, A. S., & Pinheiro, P. G. (2011). Fiedler's contingency theory: Practical application of the least preferred coworker (LPC) Scale. *IUP Journal Of Organizational Behavior, 10*(4), 7-26. Retrieved from https://www.researchgate.net/publication/258974230_Fiedler

's_Contingency_Theory_Practical_Application_of_the_Least
_Preferred_Coworker_LPC_Scale

Dabke, D. (2016). Impact of leader's emotional intelligence and transformational behavior on perceived leadership effectiveness: A multiple source view. *Business Perspectives & Research*, *4*(1), 27-40. doi:10.1177/2278533715605433

DeFrank-Cole, L., Latimer, M., Neidermeyer, P. E., & Wheatly, M. G. (2016). Understanding "Why" one university's women's leadership development strategies are so effective. *Advancing Women In Leadership*, *3626-35.*

Deinert, A., Homan, A. C., Boer, D., Voelpel, S. C., & Gutermann, D. (2015). Transformational leadership sub-dimensions and their link to leaders' personality and performance. *The Leadership Quarterly*, *26*1095-1120. doi:10.1016/j.leaqua.2015.08.001

Dinh, J. E., Lord, R. G., Gardner, W. L., Meuser, J. D., Liden, R. C., & Hu, J. (2014). Leadership theory and research in the new millennium: Current theoretical trends and changing perspectives. *The Leadership Quarterly*, *25*(Leadership Quarterly 25th Anniversary Issue), 36-62. doi:10.1016/j.leaqua.2013.11.005

Deschamps, C., Rinfret, N., Lagacé, M. C., & Privé, C. (2016). Transformational leadership and change: how leaders influence their followers' motivation through organizational justice. *Journal of Healthcare Management / American College Of Healthcare Executives*, *61*(3), 194-213.

Dew, D., Enriquez, M., McFarlane, F., & Schroeder, F. (2011). How do we lead when change is constant? *Journal of Rehabilitation,* *77*(4), 4-12. Retrieved from http://interwork.sdsu.edu/drupal/system/files/Journal%20of%20Rehabilitation%20Vol%2077%20Num%204.pdf

Dionne, S. D., Gupta, A., Sotak, K. L., Shirreffs, K. A., Serban, A., Hao, C., & Yammarino, F. J. (2014). A 25-year perspective on levels of analysis in leadership research. *The Leadership Quarterly*, *25*(1), 6–35. doi: doi.org/10.1016/j.leaqua.2013.11.002

Dinh, J. E., Lord, R. G., Gardner, W. L., Meuser, J. D., Liden, R. C., & Hu, J. (2014). Leadership theory and research in the new millennium: Current theoretical trends and changing perspectives. *The Leadership Quarterly*, *25*(Leadership Quarterly 25th Anniversary Issue), 36-62. doi:10.1016/j.leaqua.2013.11.005

Doe, R., Ndinguri, E., & Phipps, S. A. (2015). Emotional intelligence: The link to success and failure of leadership. *Academy of Educational Leadership Journal*, *19*(3), 105-114. Retrieved from https://www.questia.com/library/.../emotional-intelligence-the-link-to-success-and-failure

Donnelly, J. P. (2017). A systematic review of concept mapping dissertations. *Evaluation And Program Planning, 60*186-193. doi:10.1016/j.evalprogplan.2016.08.010

Drago-Severson, E. (2012). New opportunities for principal leadership: Shaping school
climates for enhanced teacher development. *Teachers College Record, 114* (3),
1-44. Retrieved from http://www.itcrecord.org

Dries, N., & Pepermans, R. (2012). How to identify leadership potential: Development and testing of a consensus model. *Human Resource Management, 51*(3), 361-385. doi:10.1002/hrm.21473

Edelman. (2015). 2015 Annual Edelman Trust Barometer. Retrieved from http://www.edelman.com/insights/intellectual-property/2015-edelman-trust-barometer/trust-and-innovation-edelman-trust-barometer/executive-summary/

Edmonds, A., & Kennedy, T. (2017). *An Applied Guide to Research designs: Quantitative, qualitative, and mixed methods* (2nd ed.). Thousand Oaks, CA: Sage.

Ejene, E., & Abasilim, U. (2013). Impact of transactional and transformational leadership styles on organizational performance: Empirical evidence from Nigeria. *The Journal of Commerce,* 5(1), 30-41. Retrieved from joc.hcc.edu.pk/articlepdf/5_5_1_30_41.pdf

Elqadri, Z. M., Priyono, Suci, R. P., & Chandra, T. (2015). Effect of leadership style, motivation, and giving incentives on the performance of employees. *International Education Studies,* 8(10), 183-192.

Eisenbeiss, S. A., & Van Knippenberg, D. (2015). On ethical leadership impact: The role of follower mindfulness and moral emotions. *Journal of Organizational Behavior, 36*(2), 182-195. doi:10.1002/job.1968

Emery, C., & Barker, K. (2007). The effect of transactional and transformational leadership styles on the organizational commitment and job satisfaction of customer contact personnel. *Journal of Organizational Culture, Communications & Conflict, 11*(1), 77-90.

Epitropaki, O., & Martin, R. (2013). Transformational-transactional leadership and upward influence: The role of relative leader-member exchange (RLMX) and perceived organizational support (POS). *Leadership Quarterly, 24*(2), 299-315. doi: 10.1016/j.leaqua.2012.11.007

Ereh, C., Isong, U., & Bassey, M. (2013). Transformational leadership practices of demonstrating high performance expectation and excellence in the management of personnel by secondary school principals. *Journal of Studies in Education, 3*(1), 169-176. doi:10.5296/jse.v3i1.2857

Faerman, S., McGrath, M., Quinn, R. & St. Clair, L. (2007). *Becoming a master manager: A competing values approach* (4th ed.) Hoboken, NJ: John Wiley & Sons

Farrell, M. (2016). Transparency. *Journal of Library Administration, 56*(4), 444-452. doi:10.1080/01930826.2016.1157426

Ferri-Reed, J. (2012). Managing Millennials. *Journal For Quality & Participation, 35*(2), 1. Retrieved from http://asq.org/pub/jqp/

Fleenor, J. W. (2011). Trait approach to leadership. *Encyclopedia of Industrial and Organizational Psychology, 1*(1), 831-833. doi:10.13140/2.1.3091.2804

Focht, A., & Ponton, M. (2015). Identifying primary characteristics of servant leadership: Delphi study. *International Journal of Leadership Studies, 9*(1), 44-61.

Fowler, F. (2014). *Survey research methods (Applied social research methods)* (5th ed.). Thousand Oaks, CA: Sage.

Gandhi, J., & Przeworski, A. (2013). Authoritarian institutions and the survival of autocrats. *Comparative Political Studies, 40*(11), 1279-1301.

Garcia, M., Duncan, P., Carmody-Bubb, M., & Ree, M. J. (2014). You have what? Personality! Traits that predict leadership styles for elementary principals. *Psychology*, *5*(3), 204-212. doi:10.4236/psych.2014.53031

George, B., & Sims, P. (2007). *True North: Discover your authentic leadership.* San Francisco, CA: Wiley.

Gill, C. (2012). The role of leadership in successful international mergers and acquisitions: Why Renault-Nissan succeeded and DaimlerChrysler-Mitsubishi failed. *Human Resource Management*, *51*(3), 433-456. doi:10.1002/hrm.21475

Giltinane, C. L. (2013). Leadership styles and theories. *Nursing Standard*, *27*(41), 35-39 5p. Retrieved from https://rcni.com/nursing-standard/evidence-and-practice/clinical/leadership-styles-and-theories-16616

Goodnight, R. (2011). Laissez-faire leadership. In *Encyclopedia of leadership*, (pp. 16). Thousand Oaks, CA: Sage Publications.

Gore, R. (2004). Who were the phoenicians? *National Geographic, 206*(4), 26-49.

Grabo, A., & Van Vugt, M. (2016). Original Article: Charismatic leadership and the evolution of cooperation. *Evolution And Human Behavior*, *37*399-406. doi:10.1016/j.evolhumbehav.2016.03.005

Gray, D. (2013). The value of being a safety coach most of the time. *Professional Safety, 58*(8), 20-21. Retrieved from http://www.action-learning.com/the-value-of-being-a-safety-coach-most-of-the-time/

Greenleaf, R. K. (1970). *The servant as leader.* Indianapolis, IN: The Robert K. Greenleaf Center.

Gregoire, M. B., & Arendt, S. W. (2014). Research: Leadership: Reflections over the past 100 Years. *Journal of the Academy of Nutrition and Dietetics, 114*(Supplement), S10-S19. doi:10.1016/j.jand.2014.02.023

Groves, K., & LaRocca, M. (2011). An empirical study of leader ethical values, transformational and transactional leadership, and follower attitudes toward corporate social responsibility. *Journal of Business Ethics, 103*(4), 511-528. doi:10.1007/s10551-011-0877-y

Groves, K., & LaRocca, M. (2011). Responsible leadership outcomes via stakeholder CSR values: Testing a values-centered model of transformational leadership. *Journal of Business Ethics,* 9837-55. doi:10.1007/s10551-011-1019-2

Grunewald, D., & Salleh, M. (2013). Organizational leadership - the strategic role of the chief exec. *Journal of Leadership, Accountability and Ethics, 10*(5), 9-20.

Retrieved from http://www.na-businesspress.com/JLAE/salleh_abstract.html

Gu, W. (2014, Oct 19). Executive talent search focuses on adaptive leadership; egon zehnder chairman says today's workers shun the authoritative approach. *Wall Street Journal (Online)* Retrieved from https://www.wsj.com/articles/boss-talk-asia-executive-talent-search-focuses-on-adaptive-leadership-1413751711

Gupta, V., & Singh, S. (2013). How leaders impact employee creativity: A study of Indian R&D laboratories. *Management Research Review, 36*(1), 66-88. doi: 10.1108/01409171311284594

Haber-Curran, P., & Tillapaugh, D. (2013). Leadership learning through student-centered and inquiry-focused approaches to teaching adaptive leadership. *Journal of Leadership Education, 12*(1), 92-116. Retrieved from http://www.journalofleadershiped.org/index.php/vol-12-iss-1/44-leadership-learning-through-student-centered-and-inquiry-focused-approaches-to-teaching-adaptive-leadership

Hamm, J. (2011). *Unusually excellent: The necessary nine skills required for the practice of great leadership.* San Francisco, CA: Jossey-Bass.

Hargis, M. B., Watt, J. D., Piotrowski, C. (2011). Developing leaders: Examining the role of transactional and transformational leadership across business contexts. *Organization Development Journal 29*(3), 51-66.

Hartman, J. L., & McCambridge, J. (2011). Optimizing millennials' communication Styles. *Business Communication Quarterly*, *74*(1), 22-44. doi:10.1177/1080569910395564

Hartnell, C. A., Kinicki, A. J., Lambert, L. S., Fugate, M., & Doyle Corner, P. (2016). Do similarities or differences between CEO leadership and organizational culture have a more positive effect on firm performance? A test of competing predictions. *Journal Of Applied Psychology*, *101*(6), 846-861. doi:10.1037/apl0000083

Harvey, M. J., & Harvey, M. G. (2014). Privacy and security issues for mobile health platforms. *Journal of The Association For Information Science & Technology*, 65(7), 1305-1318. doi:10.1002/asi.23066

Hauserman, C., Ivankova, N., & Stick, S. (2013). Teacher perceptions of principals' leadership qualities: A mixed methods study. *Journal of School Leadership*, 23(1), 34-63. Retrieved from http://www.rowanlittlefield.com

Heifetz, R. A. (1994). *Leadership without easy answers. [electronic resource].* Cambridge, MA : Belknap Press of Harvard University Press, 1994.

Hershey, P., & Blanchard, K. H. (1969). Management of organizational behavior. *Academy of Management Journal, 12*(4), 526. doi:10.5465/AMJ.1969.19201155

Hesse, E. D. (2013, April, 26). Servant leadership: A path to high performance. *The Washington Post.* Retrieved from http://www.washingtonpost.com/ business/capitalbusiness/servant-leadership-a-path-to-high-performance/2013/04/26/435e58b2-a7b8-11e2-8302-3c7e0ea97057_story.html

Hitt, M., Hoskisson, R. & Ireland, R. (2012). Strategic management: Concepts and cases: Competitiveness and globalization. Mason, Ohio: South-Western.

Hoffman, B. J., Woehr, D. J., Maldagen-Youngjohn, R., & Lyons, B. D. (2011). Great man or great myth? A quantitative review of the relationship between individual differences and leader effectiveness. *Journal of Occupational & Organizational Psychology, 84*(2), 347-381. doi:10.1348/096317909X485207

Hollenbeck, J., DeRue, D., & Nahrgang, J. (2015). The opponent process theory of leadership succession. *Organizational Psychology Review, 5*(4), 333-363. doi: 10.1177/2041386614530606

House, R. J. (1996). Path-goal theory of leadership: Lessons, legacy and a reformulated theory. *The Leadership Quarterly*, *7*(3), 323-352. doi:10.1016/S1048-9843(96)90024-7

House, R. J. (1977). *A 1976 theory of charismatic leadership.* In J. G. Hunt & L. L. Larsen (Eds.), *Leadership: The cutting edge.* Carbondale, IL: Southern Illinois University Press.

Hoyt, C. L., & Murphy, S. E. (2016). Managing to clear the air: Stereotype threat, women, and leadership. *The Leadership Quarterly*, *27*(Special Issue: Gender and Leadership), 387-399. doi:10.1016/j.leaqua.2015.11.002

Huang, J., Li, W., Qiu, C., Yim, F. H., & Wan, J. (2016). The impact of CEO servant leadership on firm performance in the hospitality industry. *International Journal of Contemporary Hospitality Management*, *28*(5), 945-968. doi:10.1108/IJCHM-08-2014-0388

Hughes, R., Curphy, G. & Ginnett, R. (2015). *Leadership: Enhancing the lessons of experience* (8th ed.). New York, NY: McGraw-Hill Irwin.

Humphrey, R. H. (2013). *Effective leadership: Theory, cases, and applications.* Thousand Oaks, CA: SAGE.

Ishikawa, J. (2012). Transformational leadership and gatekeeping leadership: The roles of
norm for maintaining consensus and shared leadership in team performance. *Asia Pacific Journal of Management, 29*(2), 265-283. doi:10.1007/s10490-012-9282-z

Kaifi, B., Nafei, W., Khanfar, N., & Kaifi, M. (2012). A multi-generational workforce: managing and understanding millennials. *International Journal of Business and Management, 24.* doi: http://dx.doi.org/10.5539/ijbm.v7n24p88

Kaigh, E., Driscoll, M., Tucker, E., & Lam, S. (2014). Preparing to lead: Finance professionals are essential in narrowing leadership gaps. *Corporate Finance Review, 19*(2), 5-12. Retrieved from https://www.apqc.org/knowledge-base/documents/preparing-lead-finance-professionals-are-essential-narrowing-leadership-gap

Kamisan, A. P., & King, B. E. M. (2013). Transactional and transformational leadership: A comparative study of the difference between Tony Fernandes (AirAsia) and Idris Jala (Malaysia Airlines) leadership styles from 2005-2009. *International Journal of Business and Management, 8*(24), 107-116. doi:10.5539/ijbm.v8n24p107

Kellerman, B. (2013). Leading questions: The end of leadership—Redux. *Leadership*, *9*(1), 135-139. doi: 10.1177/1742715012455132

Khan, M., Ramzan, M., Ahmed, I., & Nawaz, M. (2011). Transformational, transactional and laissez-faire styles of teaching faculty as predictors of satisfaction, and extra effort among the students: Evidence from higher education institutions. *Interdisciplinary Journal of Research in Business,* *1*, 130-135. Retrieved from http://www.idjrb.com/articlepdf/idjrbjournal131.pdf

Koenig, M., & Srikantaiah, T. (2004). *Knowledge management lessons learned; What works and what doesn't.* Medford, NJ: Information Today.

Kosicek, P. M., Soni, R., Sandbothe, R., & Slack, F. (2012). Leadership styles, industry fit, and quality focus. *Competition Forum, 10*(2), 49-54

Kouzes, J., & Posner, B. (2016). *Learning leadership: The five fundamentals of becoming an exemplary leader*. San Francisco: Wiley.

Kouzes, J., & Posner, B. (2017). *Leadership challenge* (6th ed.). Hoboken: Wiley.

Kovjanic, S., Schuh, S. C., Jonas, K., Quaquebeke, N., & Dick, R. (2012). How do transformational leaders foster positive employee outcomes? A self-determination-based analysis of employees' needs as mediating links. How do transformational leaders foster positive employee outcomes? A self-determination-based analysis of. *Journal of Organizational Behavior,* *33*(8), 1031-1052. doi: 10.1002/job.1771.

Krishnan, V. R. (2012). Transformational leadership and personal outcomes: Empowerment as mediator. *Leadership & Organization Development Journal,* *33*(6), 550-563. doi: 10.1108/01437731211253019

Kundeliene, K., & Leitoniene, S. (2015). Business information transparency: Causes and evaluation possibilities. *Procedia - Social and Behavioral Sciences,* *213*(20th International Scientific Conference "Economics and Management 2015 (ICEM-2015)"), 340-344. doi:10.1016/j.sbspro.2015.11.548

Latham, J. R. (2014). Leadership for quality and innovation: challenges, theories, and a framework for future research. *Quality Management Journal, 21*(1), 11-15. Retrieved from Retrieved from http://www.academia.edu/6106466/Leadership_for_Quality_ and_Innovation_Challenges_Theories_and_a_Framework_fo r_Future_Research

Lee, Y. (2011). A comparison of leadership behaviors in the financial industry in the United States and Taiwan. *Journal of International Management Studies, 6*(2), 1-12. Retrieved from www.jimsjournal.org/5%20Yueh-shian%20Lee.pdf

Liden, R. C., Wayne, S. J., Chenwei, L., & Meuser, J. D. (2014). Servant leadership and serving culture: influence on individual and unit performance. *Academy of Management Journal, 57*(5), 1434-1452. doi:10.5465/amj.2013.0034

Lilian, S. C. (2014). Virtual Teams: Opportunities and challenges for e-leaders. *Procedia - Social and Behavioral Sciences, 110*(The 2-dn International scientific conference contemporary issues in business, Management and Education 2013"), 1251-1261. doi:10.1016/j.sbspro.2013.12.972

Ling, Y., Simsek, Z., Lubatkin, M. H., & Veiga, J. F. (2008). The impact of transformational CEOs on the performance of small- to medium-sized firms: Does organizational context matter? *Journal of Applied Psychology, 93*(4), 923-934. doi:10.1037/0021-9010.93.4.923

Lord, R. G., Day, D. V., Zaccaro, S. J., Avolio, B. J., & Eagly, A. H. (2017). Leadership in applied psychology: Three waves of theory and research. *Journal Of Applied Psychology, 102*(3), 434-451. doi:10.1037/apl0000089

Lyons, S., Ng, E., & Schweitzer, L. (2014). Changing demographics and the shifting nature of careers: implications for research and human resource development. *Human Resource Development Review, 13*(2), 181-206. doi: 10.1177/1534484314524201

MacDonald, H., & Luque, M. S. (2013). *Path-Goal Theory of Leadership.* Sage Publications, Inc. doi: 10.4135/9781452276090

Maltby, E. (2009, February 25). Small biz loan failure rate hits 12%. *CNNMoney.com.* Retrieved from http://money.cnn.com/2009/02/25/smallbusiness/smallbiz_lo an_defaults_soar.smb/

Marques, J. (2010). Spiritual considerations for managers: What matters most to workforce members in challenging times. *Journal of Business Ethics, 97*(3), 381-390. doi10.1007/s10551-010-0514-1

Marshall, B., Cardon, P., Poddar, A., & Fontenot, R. (2013). Does sample size matter in qualitative research?: A review of qualitative interviews in is research. *Journal of Computer Information Systems, 54*(1), 11-22.

Martínez-Córcoles, M., & Stephanou, K. (2017). Linking active transactional leadership and safety performance in military operations. *Safety Science, 96*93-101. doi:10.1016/j.ssci.2017.03.013

Mazurkiewicz, G. (2012). Leadership and mental models. Study of school principals' awareness. *Zarzadzanie Publiczne,* (20), 27-48. Retrieved from http://www.ejournals.eu/Zarzadzanie-Publiczne/2012/Zarzadzanie-Publiczne-4-2012/art/1432/

McCleskey, J. (2014). Situational, transformational, and transactional leadership and leadership development. *Journal of Business Studies Quarterly, 5*(4), 117-130. Retrieved from http://jbsq.org/archives/.

McLean, G. N., & Beigi, M. (2016). The importance of worldviews on women's leadership to HRD. *Advances In Developing Human Resources, 18*(2), 260-270. doi:10.1177/1523422316641419

Meuser, J. D., Gardner, W. L., Dinh, J. E., Hu, J., Liden, R. C., & Lord, R. G. (2016). A network analysis of leadership theory. *Journal of Management, 42*(5), 1374. doi:10.1177/0149206316647099

Meyer, J. P. (2013). The science-practice gap and employee engagement: It's a matter of principle. *Canadian Psychology, 54*(4), 235-245. doi: 10.1037/a0034521

Moreno, P., & McLean, G. N. (2016). Women leaders in a predominantly male-dominated society. *Advances In Developing Human Resources, 18*(2), 152-168. doi:10.1177/1523422316641400

Morgan, L., Paucar-Caceres, A., & Wright, G. (2014). Leading effective global virtual teams: The consequences of methods of communication. *Systemic Practice & Action Research, 27*(6), 607-624. doi:10.1007/s11213-014-9315-2

Naicker, I., Chikoko, V., & Mthiyane, S. (2014). Instructional leadership practices in challenging school contexts. Education as Change, 18S137-S150. doi:10.1080/16823206.2014.865999

Neubert, M. J., Hunter, E. M., & Tolentino, R. C. (2016). A servant leader and their stakeholders: When does organizational structure enhance a leader's influence? *Leadership Quarterly, 27*(6), 896-910. doi:10.1016/j.leaqua.2016.05.005

Nohria, N., & Khurana, R., Editors (2010), *Handbook of leadership theory and practice*, A Harvard business school centennial colloquium, Harvard Business Press, Boston, Massachusetts.

Northouse, P. (2013). *Leadership: Theory and practice.* (6th ed.). Thousand Oaks, CA: Sage Publications.

Omilion-Hodges, L. M., & Wieland, S. B. (2016). Unraveling the leadership dichotomy in the classroom and beyond. *Journal of Leadership Education,* *15*(1), 110-128. doi:1012806/V15/I1/A3

Onorato, M. (2013). Transformational leadership style in the education sector: An empirical study of corporate managers and educational leaders. *Academy of Educational Leadership Journal,* *17*(1), 33-47. Retrieved from http://www.alliedacademies.org/academy-of-educational-leadership-journal/volume-issue.php?volume=Volume%2017,%20Issue%201&year=2013&journal=aelj

O'Reilly, M., & Parker, N. (2013). 'Unsatisfactory saturation': A critical exploration of the notion of saturated sample sizes in qualitative research. *Qualitative Research,* 13(2), 190-197. doi:10.1177/1468794112446106

Otte, S. (2015). Implementing a Dominican Model of Leadership. *Educational Considerations,* *43*(1), 4-12.

Partida, B. (2015). Using dynamic leadership to prepare for the future. *Supply Chain Management Review,* *19*(4), 54-56

Phillips, A. S., & Phillips, C. R. (2016). Behavioral styles of path-goal theory: An exercise for developing leadership skills. *Management Teaching Review,* 1(3), 148. doi:10.1177/2379298116639725

Pongpearchan, P. (2016). Effect of transformational leadership on strategic human resource management and firm success of Toyota's dealer in Thailand. *Journal of Business & Retail Management Research, 10*(2), 53-63. Retrieved from http://www.scmr.com/article/using_dynamic_leadership_to_prepare_for_the_future

Porter, E. (2012, July 10). The spreading scourge of corporate corruption. *New York Times.* Retrieved from http://www.nytimes.com/2012/07/11/business/ economy/the-spreading-scourge-of-corporate-corruption.html?_r=0

Posner, B. Z., Crawford, B., & Denniston-Stewart, R. (2015). A longitudinal study of canadian student leadership practices. *Journal of Leadership Education, 14*(2), 161-181. doi:10.12806/V14/I2/R11

Press, M., & Arnould, E. J. (2014). Narrative transparency. *Journal of Marketing Management, 30*(13-14), 1353-1376. doi:10.1080/0267257X.2014.925958

Qu, R., Janssen, O., & Shi, K. (2015). Transformational leadership and follower creativity: The mediating role of follower relational identification and the moderating role of leader creativity expectations. *The Leadership Quarterly, 26*286-299. doi:10.1016/j.leaqua.2014.12.004

Ravazadeh, N., & Ravazadeh, A. (2013). The effect of transformational leadership on staff empowerment. *International Journal of Business and Social Science, 4*(10) Retrieved from ijbssnet.com/journals/Vol_4_No_10_Special_Issue_August_ 2013/20.pdf

Rietsema, K. W., & Watkins, D. V. (2012). Beyond leadership. *International Journal of Business & Social Science*, *3*(4), 22- 30. Retrieved from http://www.ijbssnet.com/update/

Robinson, M. A., & Boies, K. (2016). Different ways to get the job done: Comparing the effects of intellectual stimulation and contingent reward leadership on task-related outcomes. *Journal of Applied Social Psychology*, *46*(6), 336-353. doi:10.1111/jasp.12367

Roof, R. (2015). The association of individual spirituality on employee engagement: The spirit at work. *130*(3), 585-599. doi:10.1007/s10551-014-2246-0

Rowold, J. (2014). Instrumental leadership: Extending the transformational-transactional leadership paradigm. *Zeitschrift Für Personalforschung*, *28*(3), 367-390. doi:10.1688/ZfP-2014-03-Rowold

Rowold, J. (2011). Relationship between leadership behaviors and performance: *The Leadership & Organization Development Journal, 32,* 628-647. doi: 10.1108/01437731111161094

Sabnis, S., & Charles, D. (2012). Opportunities and challenges: Security in ehealth. Bell Labs Technical Journal, 17(3), 105-111. doi:10.1002/bltj.21561

Saccomano, S. J., & Pinto-Zipp, G. (2011). Registered nurse leadership style and confidence in delegation. *Journal of Nursing Management,* *19*(4), 522-533. doi:10.1111/j.1365-2834.2010.01189.x

Safferstone, M. J. (2005). Organizational leaderships: Classic works and contemporary perspectives. *Choice: Current Reviews for Academic Libraries, 42*(6), 959.

Sarros, J. C., & Sarros, A. M. (2011). Five years on: leadership challenges of an experienced CEO. *School Leadership & Management,* *31*(3), 235-260. doi:10.1080/13632434.2011.587406

Savolainen, T. (2014). Trust-building in e-leadership: a case study of leaders' challenges and skills in technology-mediated interaction. *Journal of Global Business Issues, 8*(2), 45-56. Retrieved from https://www.highbeam.com/doc/1P3-3587934011.html

Schoel, C., Bluemke, M., Mueller, P., & Stahlberg, D. (2011). When autocratic leaders become an option—Uncertainty and self-esteem predict implicit leadership preferences. *Journal of Personality and Social Psychology*, *101*(3), 521-540. doi:10.1037/a0023393

Schuh, S. C., Zhang, X., & Tian, P. (2013). For the good or the bad? Interactive effects of transformational leadership with moral and authoritarian leadership behaviors. *Journal of Business Ethics,* *116*(3), 629-640. doi:http://dx.doi.org/10.100 7/s10551-012-1486-0

Silva, A. (2014). What do we really know about leadership? *Journal Of Business Studies Quarterly*, *5*(4), 1-4. Retrieved from http://jbsq.org/wp-content/uploads/2014/06/June_2014_1.pdf

Simmons, K., Carpenter, L., Dyal, A., Austin, S., & Shumack, K. (2012). Preparing transformational leaders: Three collaborative initiatives. *Education*, 132(4), 754-763. Retrieved from http://www.projectinnovation.b12/index/html

Sindell, T., & Shamberger, S. (2016). Beyond gender: Changing the leadership conversation. *People & Strategy*, *39*(3), 32-35. Retrieved from https://www.c4x.com/website/_pages/resources.cfm

Smothers, J. (2011). Assumption-based leadership: A historical post-hoc conceptualization of the assumptions underlying leadership styles. *Journal of Applied Management and Entrepreneurship*, 16(3), 44-59. Retrieved from https://www.greenleaf-publishing.com/journals/journal-of-applied-management-entrepreneurship

Srinivasan, S. K. (2010). Handbook of leadership theory and practice: A Harvard business school centennial colloquium on advancing leadership. *Vikalpa: The Journal for Decision Makers*, 35(4), 122-129.

Stewart, J. S., Oliver, E. G., Cravens, K. S., & Oishi, S. (2016). Managing millennials: Embracing generational differences. *Business Horizons*, doi:10.1016/j.bushor.2016.08.011

Stogdill, R. M. (1950). Leadership, membership and organization. *Psychological Bulletin*, 47(1), 1-14. doi:10.1037/h0053857

Stoker, J. I., Grutterink, H., & Kolk, N. J. (2012). Do transformational CEOs always make the difference? The role of TMT feedback seeking behavior. *Leadership Quarterly*, 23(3), 582-592. doi:10.1016/j.leaqua.2011.12.009

Sudha, K. S., Shahnawaz, M. G., & Farhat, A. (2016). Leadership styles, leader's effectiveness and well-being: Exploring collective efficacy as a mediator. *Vision (09722629)*, 20(2), 111-120. doi:10.1177/0972262916637260

Thompson, J. (2012). Transformational leadership can improve workforce competencies. *Nursing Management, 18*(10), 21-24. doi: 10.7748/nm2012.03.18.10.21.c8958

Torres, R., & Reeves, M. (2014). Adaptive leadership. *Leadership Excellence, 28*(7), 8. doi: 10.1002/9781119204084.ch4

Tyler, L. S. (2015). Emotional intelligence: Not just for leaders. *American Journal Of Health-System Pharmacy: AJHP: Official Journal of The American Society Of Health-System Pharmacists, 72*(21), 1849. doi:10.2146/ajhp150750

United States Army. (2006). *Army leadership manual: Field manual 6-22.* Washington, DC: Headquarters, Department of the Army. Retrieved from http://www.fas.org/irp/doddir/army/fm6-22.pdf

Van Dierendonck, D., & I. Nuijten. 2011. The servant leadership survey: Development and validation of a multidimensional measure. *Journal of Business and Psychology* 26, no. 3:249-267. Retrieved from https://www.ncbi.nlm.nih.gov/pmc/articles/PMC3152712/

Wang, V. X. (2012). *E–Leadership in the New Century*. IGI Global. Encyclopedia of e-leadership, counseling and training. 2012, v. 1, p12-22. Retrieved from http://www.igi-global.com/chapter/leadership-new-century/58424

Welch, J. (2013, June 19). Insights on charismatic leadership from the heroes and villains. leadership by the people.org. Retrieved from http://www.leadershipbythepeople.org/Charismatic-Political-Leaders.php

Whitenack, D., & Swanson, P. (2013). The transformative potential of boundary spanners: A narrative inquiry into preservice teacher education and professional development in an NCLB-impacted context. Education Policy Analysis Archives, 21(55-57), 1-16. doi:10.1007/0003278469187381

Willis, D. G., Sullivan-Bolyai, S., Knafl, K., & Cohen, M. Z. (2016). Distinguishing Features and Similarities Between Descriptive Phenomenological and Qualitative Description Research. *Western Journal of Nursing Research*, *38*(9), 1185-1204. doi:10.1177/0193945916645499

Winkler, I. (2010). Contemporary leadership theories; Enhancing the understanding of the complexity, subjectivity, and the dynamics of leadership. Heidelberg, New York: Physica-Verlag.

Yang, I. (2015). Positive effects of laissez-faire leadership: conceptual exploration. *Journal of Management Development*, *34*(10), 1246-1261. doi:10.1108/JMD-02-2015-0016

Yates, J., & Leggett, T. (2016). Qualitative research: An introduction. *Radiologic Technology*, *88*(2), 225-231. Retrieved from www.radiologictechnology.org/content/88/2/225.full

Yukl, G. (2012). Leadership in organizations. (8th ed.). Upper Saddle, NJ: Pearson Prentice Hall.

Zaech, S., & Baldegger, U. (2017). Leadership in start-ups. *International Small Business Journal*, *35*(2), 157-177. doi:10.1177/0266242616676883

Zimmerly, J. (2016). Four keys to adaptive leadership. *Strategic Finance,* *98*(1), 19-20. Retrieved from https://www.highbeam.com/doc/1G1-458164805.html

Zdaniuk, A., & Bobocel, D. R. (2015). The role of idealized influence leadership in promoting workplace forgiveness. *The Leadership Quarterly*, *26*863-877. doi:10.1016/j.leaqua.2015.06.008

ABOUT THE AUTHOR

Dr. Warren Martin earned his Ph.D. in Business Administration and Organizational Leadership from North Central University and his MBA from the University of Michigan *(Go Blue)*. During a 21-year career in the United States Army he served in the Infantry, Military Police, and Special Forces *(Green Berets)*.

After he retired from the Army he transitioned to business, working for Domino's Pizza Corporation and later was a Domino's franchise business owner. Upon earning his MBA and Ph.D. he transitioned to teaching at Norwich University and currently serves as the MBA program chair at Bryan University in Springfield Missouri.

Dr. Martin is a member of numerous writing organizations and is President of the Missouri Writers' Guild and past President of the St. Louis Publishers Association. He has a debut award winning novel titled "Forgotten Soldiers: What Happened to Jacob Walden." As a Grandparent he has a an award winning Children's book series based on his experiences with his grandchildren "Adventures with Pop Pop". Under the pen name Marty Martin he has a Mystery Thriller Series titled "Farmerville."

Originally from New York City, he lives with his wife, Debbie Kay, in St. Louis Missouri.

warrenmartinleadership.com

LEADERSHIP

www.ingramcontent.com/pod-product-compliance
Lightning Source LLC
Chambersburg PA
CBHW060228030426
42335CB00014B/1367